Depression Era Recipes

by

Patricia R. Wagner

Depression Era Recipes

Published by Media Solution Services
440 Park Avenue South.
New York, NY 10016

Illustrations, book and cover design by
Patricia R. Wagner,
Stanchfield, MN 55080

Cover Illustration by Gene Kadlac,
Brooklyn Park, MN 55445

Printed and bound
through Pac-com Korea, Inc.

Seventeenth Printing August 1999
Eighteenth Printing January 2000
Nineteenth Printing July 2000
Twentieth Printing August 2001
Twenty-first Printing July 2002

Acknowledgements

The recipes contained in this book were for the most part obtained from brittle, hand-written recipe books composed by relatives and friends' relatives. When this project was started, old recipe books began coming out of the woodwork. The women who wrote these cookbooks, and their children, lived through the Depression: they learned to be savers, which accounts for the existence of the books.

The Depression wasn't all soup lines and poverty. The information related herein is intended to show how people coped with the Depression, their diversions and what life was all about, what they had and how they spent their leisure time. Not all of these recipes have been personally tested by the author. But if they were good enough for Gramma Signe, Aunt Minnie and Mom, they're good enough for us.

This wasn't just a matter of typing up old recipes. There was an incredible amount of research involved. I learned so much from this effort that it was like taking a history class. Enjoy! It's a regular walk down memory lane. Forget the microwave. Let's get back to the way Grandma cooked.

I would like to thank my mom, Ruth Wagner, and Maureen O'Neill, Betty Hendrickson, Diane Wagner, Dorothy McGrath Hess, Ruby Beckman, Kitty Bakken, Sharon Rudquist and Elaine Nilsen for all they did to help. They trusted me with precious family cookbooks, which were upwards of sixty years old and quite fragile. Their generosity made this book possible. Other thanks go to the folks at the East Central Regional Library in Cambridge, MN, who were so kind in helping me find resource materials and who answered so many of my obscure questions...always with a smile.

TABLE OF CONTENTS

Hope

There's a new moon tonight, and so I wonder
If you will see it - and if it will start
Some vague regret for all the crashing thunder
Of bitter phrases rooted from the heart;
Is it not strange when pride has cooled down
How one can miss a glance - a touch of hand -
And how the timid bow-boy that we ruled down
Can raise his havoc with the peace we planned?

How do you spend your time - are you pursuing
The fevered lures that help you to forget,
Or like a certain lad - are you renewing
Your joust with grief thru nights so black?

There's a new moon tonight - perhaps you'll see
Its radiance - and muse a bit on me!

-Don Wahn, 1933

This poem was discovered in my father's dresser drawer (the one with the treasures in it) shortly after his death on April 1, 1989. Dad apparently was impressed by the hope this poem inspired, as he kept it under lock and key all these years.

How to Tell Who Lived During the Depression

You can always tell Depression Survivors by what they save: First of all, money - whenever they can. Then, and not necessarily in this order, they save: paper bags, bottles and jars, string, rubber bands (in Minnesota we call them rubber binders), twist ties, newspapers and magazines, any paper that's blank on one side, coupons, bread bags (they wash them and hang them inside out on the clothesline to dry,) seeds from vegetables to grow in the garden next year, leftover food, Cool Whip bowls and prescription medication containers, all sorts of clothing, and anything else that they may have a purpose for later.

Another giveaway is the phrases they use. Perhaps the most common one is, "Don't throw it away - it's still <u>good</u>!" Others you may identify with: "For that price you could have bought a new one!" "How much? Boy, they sure saw <u>you</u> coming!" "You can fix that." "You can make it yourself lots cheaper!" "Keep it...you might need it someday." And of course, "Clean your plate!"

If these phrases don't sneak into their vocabulary, you can tell Depression Survivors by observing their habits: They turn out the light when they leave a room, they shut off the water while brushing their teeth, they don't use the clothes dryer from April to October. They have always worn sensible shoes, they have a garden and do a lot of canning, they turn down the heat at night. They probably don't have an air conditioner, but they most likely have a microwave and use it for warming up the morning's coffee. They write their grocery lists in pencil on the backs of old envelopes; they can forecast the weather using only their knees and they doubt the credibility of color radar. They buy things on sale if at all possible. You've seen them - they're the ones with the good old toasters and the window fans that work.

Considering the tremendous changes that these folks have experienced over the past 50-60 years, it is no wonder that they cling to the ways of the past. We can learn a lot from these wonderful people. It might be a good idea to bring back some of the frugal habits of our senior citizens. "Just think of the money you'll save!!"

Breakfasts

Dinner may be pleasant,
So may social tea;
But yet, me thinks the breakfast
Is good enough for me.

That's an Old Idea

Modern diet starts by *tempting* the appetite

*That is why the world has turned to these unique grain foods,
so amazingly delicious that you forget they're good for you,
and eat them because they taste good when nothing else does*

HERE are crunchy grains that taste like toasted nutmeats . . . only richer. They're made from whole wheat. Approximately 20% is bran. But you would never guess it, so delightfully is it concealed.

They have a flavor, a richness that once you taste, you never forget. They are as enticing as confections. To millions they have brought a new conception of a cereal dish. There is no other like them.

Each grain is steam puffed, then oven crisped. A process applied to but this one food in the world. Every food cell is broken to make digestion easy. Each grain is eight times its normal size. You eat them because you love them, not because they are "good for you."

And that is the right way to get the food elements which you need. Modern diet starts by *tempting* the appetite. For foods that tempt digest better.

Just try Puffed Wheat. It will prove that the food you need can be gloriously delicious, too. Serve with milk or cream, or half and half. That adds to their delights and assures the vitamines plus the bran and good of the wheat.

Try too with fresh or cooked fruits. Give to the children in every way you can. A breakfast adventure, a luncheon change, a supper dish beyond compare. Get Quaker Puffed Wheat at your grocer.

Quaker Puffed Rice Also

Kernels of rice, steam exploded like Puffed Wheat. Each grain an adventure, delicious and enticing.

THE QUAKER OATS COMPANY

1

Spanish Omelet

2 T. butter
2 large onions
2 buttons garlic
1/2-1 pt. tomatoes
Dash red pepper
2-3 small chilies
Salt
6 eggs

Chop onions fine and brown in butter in a large skillet. Add garlic and fry for a minute or two. Add tomatoes, pepper, chilies and salt to taste. Cook all till well done. Beat eggs thoroughly, pour over tomato mixture, let brown and then fold. Serve hot. Although even when it's cold it's hot!

Muffins

3 c. flour
4 t. baking powder
2 T. sugar
1/2 t. salt
1 egg
1 1/2 c. milk
4 T. melted lard

Sift together flour, baking powder, sugar and salt. Beat egg well and stir in milk. Pour this gradually into dry ingredients and pour in melted lard. Bake in greased muffin tins in moderate oven until nicely browned. Serve with butter and preserves.

Quick Breakfast Puffs

2 eggs
1 scant cup milk
1 T. melted shortening
1 1/2 c. flour
3 t. baking powder
1/2 t. salt

Beat the eggs very thoroughly and add the milk and shortening. Sift flour, salt and baking powder twice. Add the liquid and beat for two minutes. Pour into hot, well greased muffin pans and bake for about 20 minutes in hot oven. Serve warm with butter.

Graham Gems

2 c. Graham flour
1/2 t. salt
4 t. baking powder
1 egg
1 1/4 c. milk
2 T. melted shortening

Sift together flour, salt and baking powder. Beat eggs well and stir in milk. Add shortening and mix to form batter. Bake in hot, greased gem pans in a moderately hot oven for about 20 minutes.

Graham flour is actually whole wheat flour that is so-called because it was developed by Sylvester W. Graham, an American Dietary Reformer, in 1834. Have you noticed lately S.W. Graham cereal showing up on your grocer's shelves? That's him! But they don't tell you that.

Breakfast Muffins

1 1/4 c. milk
1/4 t. salt
2 c. flour
2 T. butter, melted
2 T. sugar
1 egg
1 T. baking powder

Sift all dry ingredients together. Add milk, egg and melted butter and beat fairly well. Bake in greased muffin tins in a moderate oven for about a half hour. These are good and not too hard to prepare.

Baking Powder Biscuits

2 c. flour
4 t. baking powder
1 t. salt
2 T. lard
1 c. sweet milk

Sift dry ingredients together. Rub in lard, add milk gradually. Mix to a smooth dough, roll to 1/2" thickness. Cut with biscuit cutter. Handle as little as possible to make light, flaky biscuits. Bake in a quick oven. Grandma called these "Bakin' Powder" biscuits.

Dropped Eggs

Boiling water
Salt
2 eggs
Buttered Toast

Boil water in a shallow pan - a frying pan is good. Salt lightly and drop in the eggs, one at a time, having previously broken them into a cup to see that they are fresh. Cook till the whites are just-set, then lift from the water with a skimmer and place on hot buttered toast.

Shirred Eggs

2 eggs
1 T. butter
Salt
Pepper

Melt butter in an egg shirrer or any fireproof earthen baking dish. Break the eggs into the dish and season to taste. Cook in moderate oven till set. A little chopped parsley, cheese or a few fried bread crumbs may be sprinkled on top before baking.

1933: *The Chicago World's Fair opened, attracting more than 20 million visitors. It was so successful that it was held over for another year. Contributing to that success was Miss Sally Rand, whose performances with huge fans or an oversized bubble delighted fair-goers.*

Cheese Omelet

3 eggs
3 T. water
2 T. mild grated cheese
1/8 t. pepper
2 T. butter
Salt, if needed

Beat the eggs lightly, add water and seasoning. Melt butter in an omelet pan, pour in the eggs and stir and mix lightly till they begin to set. Sprinkle with the cheese, then scrape and push the omelet to one side of the pan. Cook about one minute, then either turn in the pan by slipping a knife under the omelet, or hold the pan for a moment in front of the fire or under the flame of the gas range. Turn onto a hot dish and serve at once.

Cheese Souffle

3 T. flour
3 T. butter
3 eggs, separated
1 c. milk
1 c. grated cheese
Salt
Pepper

Stir butter and flour together in a saucepan over fire, without browning. Add the milk, a little at a time, and stir till the mixture boils. Add cheese, salt and pepper - set aside to cool. Beat the yolks and add them to the mixture in the saucepan and blend thoroughly. Lastly, beat the egg whites to a stiff froth, fold into the mixture, and turn into a deep well-greased dish. Bake in a moderate oven about 25 minutes, and serve at once, because it soon falls and no one will be impressed.

Plain Omelet

4 eggs
4 T. water
1/4 t. salt
Pepper
2 T. butter

Beat eggs lightly, add salt, pepper and water and mix well. Melt butter in an omelet pan and allow it to become quite hot without browning. Pour in eggs and stir gently till they begin to set. Now push the omelet down to one side of the pan that it may be thick and puffy, tilting the pan to keep it at one side. Cook till just set in the center and golden brown on the side next to the pan. Turn onto a dish, brown side up, and serve plain or with tomato or other sauce. This is good.

Although farmers were hit hard by falling market prices, fortunately many had land so they could raise their own food and be fairly self-sufficient.

Scrambled Eggs

6 eggs
3 T. butter
6 T. cream or milk
1/2 t. salt
A little pepper

Beat eggs lightly, add seasoning and cream or milk, and place with butter in a saucepan. Stir constantly with a wooden spoon till it begins to thicken, then remove the pan to a cooler part of the stove and continue the cooking till the eggs are set. Serve either on buttered toast or garnished with points of toast. Some- times a little grated cheese, a few green peas or mushrooms (cooked), or a few asparagus tips are added to the eggs just before serving.

French Toast

2 eggs
1 c. milk
1/2 t. salt
1 t. vanilla
8 slices stale bread

Lightly beat eggs. Add milk, salt and vanilla. Dip bread slices into mixture so that both sides are coated. Fry in a little fat in a hot skillet until browned. Turn and brown the other side. Serve with syrup, jam or powdered sugar. A good way to use up bread that's not so fresh.

Graham Batter Cakes

1 c. flour
1 T. baking powder
1/2 t. salt
2 T. sugar
1/2 c. whole wheat flour
1 egg
1 c. milk
1 T. shortening, melted

Sift together flour, baking powder, salt and sugar. Stir in whole wheat flour. Beat the egg and add milk and shortening. Add this to the dry ingredients and beat till mixed. Pour onto hot greased griddle and cook until bubbles appear; turn and brown on other side. Turn the pancakes only once or they'll get tough. Serve hot with butter and syrup.

Ham Muffins

1-1/2 c. flour
2 t. baking powder
1 T. sugar
1/4 t. salt
1/2 c. wheat bran
3/4 c. cooked ham, ground
2 eggs
1 c. milk
3 T. melted shortening

Sift together flour, baking powder, sugar and salt. Stir in bran and ham. Beat the eggs, add milk and shortening. Add this to the dry ingredients and stir gently, only until mixed. Pour into muffin tins that have been well greased. Fill tins about 2/3 full. Bake in a moderate oven for about 25 minutes. Serve hot with butter.

Omelet

1 slice bread
1/4 c. milk
4 eggs, separated
Salt
Pepper

Soak bread in milk to soften. Beat egg yolks until light and creamy. Add seasonings and softened bread. Beat egg whites until stiff and fold into mixture. Pour into hot omelet pan or skillet and cook until set. Then put into hot oven for a few minutes to dry out the top. Serve immediately.

Swiss Eggs

1 T. butter
2 T. grated cheese
4 very thin slices
   of cheese
4 eggs
3 T. cream
Salt and Pepper

Melt butter in a shallow baking dish. Cut the cheese slices in pieces of convenient size to cover the bottom of the dish. Break eggs and drop into dish, season, and pour the cream over the eggs. Sprinkle the grated cheese on top and bake in a moderate oven until the eggs are set and the cheese is a delicate brown color.

Hard and Soft Cooked Eggs

To cook eggs so that they will be firm all the way through and yet not tough or indigestible, put them in a saucepan of boiling water, cover closely and place on part of the stove where the water will remain very hot, but not boil, and let stand for twenty minutes. To cook eggs so that they will be soft, follow the above directions, but let the eggs remain only ten minutes. It's that easy!

Eggs in Prison

2 c. cold cooked meat
4 eggs
Stale browned
   bread crumbs
Seasoning to suit
   the meat

Thoroughly grease four small cups and sprinkle thickly with the bread crumbs. Season and flavor the meat rather highly, and line the cups with it, leaving a hollow in the middle. You may want to mix a little gravy or stock with the meat if it's too dry. Break an egg into each hollow left for this purpose in each cup. Salt and pepper each serving and bake in a moderate oven till the eggs are set. Turn out onto a plate and serve with sauce or gravy if you like.

Homestead Breakfast

2 large boiled potatoes
6 slices bacon, chopped
1 onion, chopped
6 eggs
1/4 c. milk
1/2 t. salt
Pepper

Fry bacon until crisp and pour off some of the fat. Add the onion and fry for a few minutes. Dice the potatoes and add to bacon, fry until browned. Beat eggs a little, add milk, salt and pepper. Pour over potato mixture. Cook, stirring often, until eggs are set. Very filling! This will hold them till lunch!

Cooking Bacon

Although there are several ways to cook bacon, the ideal bacon is crisp, light brown in color, and delicately flavored.

Frying: Lay bacon in a cold frying pan. Place the pan over a low fire. When heated to the melting point, the fat will begin to fry out.

Then cook slowly, pouring off the excess fat from time to time. Turn frequently, increasing the heat. When the bacon is crisp and brown, it is ready to serve.

Boiling: Some prefer to cook bacon by placing it in a skillet and covering it with boiling water, placing it on the fire and boiling it until the fat has cooked away, and finishing by browning the bacon in the fat.

Oven: Lay strips of bacon in a shallow pan and place it in a hot oven, pouring off the fat from time to time. When the bacon has been browned on both sides, serve immediately.

Broiling: The ideal method of cooking bacon is to lay slices of bacon on a wire rack, placing a drip pan underneath to save the fat. Use a hot fire, and as soon as one side of the bacon is slightly brown, turn it and brown the other side.

1931: *Kate Smith's first radio broadcast was aired. People loved her and shortly she became the First Lady of Radio.*

Corn Meal Mush

1 c. corn meal
1 c. cold water
1 t. salt
4 c. boiling water

Mix together corn meal, cold water and salt. Pour boiling water into top of double boiler. Slowly stir in corn meal mixture. Cook over high heat for about 3 minutes. Cover and steam for about 20 minutes. Serve with maple syrup. If there is any left, shape into patties and fry them up for lunch.

Ham and Potato Patties

1 1/2 c. leftover
   mashed potatoes
1 egg
1 c. cooked ham, chopped
1 T. onion
A little pepper

Mix together potatoes and egg with a fork. Add ham, onion and pepper. Shape into flat patties. Dip in a little flour and fry in bacon fat or lard. Serve hot.

Breakfast Rice

4 c. rice, hot or cold
Milk
Sugar
Butter
Cinnamon

If the rice is cold, put in the top of the double boiler with the other ingredients and heat till at a nice serving temperature. If rice is hot, just add the other ingredients and mix.

Some people used to think that some other people were a little crazy to actually eat this for breakfast!

Waffles

1 c. flour
1/2 t. salt
2 t. Rumford baking powder
2 eggs, separated
1 c. milk
2 T. melted butter

Sift flour, salt and baking powder. Add egg yolks and milk and beat to make a smooth batter. Stir in melted butter, and at the last minute, fold in stiffly beaten egg whites. Bake in hot, well-greased waffle irons.

America's amiable, ambling actor, Henry Fonda, made his film debut in 1935. "Young Mr. Lincoln," 1939, was one of his most significant films of the time.

Waffles

2 c. flour
1 T. baking powder
1/2 t. salt
2 t. sugar
1 3/4 c. sour milk
2 eggs separated
1/3 c. melted shortening

Sift together the flour, baking powder, salt and sugar. Beat the egg yolks and add the milk and shortening. Stir this into the dry ingredients and beat well. Beat egg whites until stiff. Fold into batter. Pour into a hot, greased waffle iron and bake until browned. Serve hot with butter and syrup. Try some fruit on top.

Currant Breakfast Bread

1 1/2 c. flour
2 t. baking powder
1/2 t. salt
1/4 c. lard
1 c. sugar
1 egg
1/2 c. milk
1/3 c. currants
1 t. cinnamon
1 T. sugar

Sift together flour, baking powder and salt. Cream the lard and gradually add the sugar. Add egg and beat well. Add dry ingredients to this mixture, alternating with the milk. Pour into greased bread pan. Mix together currants, cinnamon and sugar - sprinkle over batter. Bake in a 350 degree oven for 25 minutes. Break into pieces and serve with butter.

One-Bowl Muffins

3 T. lard
1/4 c. sugar
2 eggs
2 c. flour
1 T. baking powder
1/2 t. salt
1 c. milk

Cream lard, add sugar and beat well. Add an egg, beat well. Add the other egg and beat well again. Stir together flour, baking powder and salt. Add to egg mixture, alternating with milk. Mix only until blended. Fill greased muffin tins about 2/3 full. Bake at 350 degrees for about 25 minutes.

Delicate Pancakes

2 T. butter
4 eggs
2 T. flour
1/2 t. salt
1 c. milk

Separate eggs, beat the whites till stiff. Beat yolks thoroughly, add flour and salt. When well mixed, stir in the milk. At the last moment, fold in the whites. Melt butter in a large skillet, pour in batter and cook over a moderately hot fire until it begins to set. Then transfer the pan to a hot oven to finish cooking. Turn onto a hot dish and serve with applesauce.

Cereal Waffles

1 c. cold cooked
   oatmeal or farina
1 c. flour
2 eggs, separated
1 c. milk
1 T. baking powder
1/2 t. salt

Sift flour, salt and baking powder. Add egg yolks, milk and cold cereal, beating well to get rid of the lumps. Beat the egg whites to a stiff froth and fold them gently into the batter. Cook at once in hot, greased waffle irons. Serve with butter and syrup or honey.

Corn Meal Waffles

1/2 c. corn meal
1 1/2 c. water
1 c. milk
3/4 c. flour
1 t. salt
1 T. baking powder
1/4 c. sugar
2 eggs

Put corn meal and water in a saucepan and cook until soft; add salt and milk and set aside to cool. Sift flour, sugar and baking powder together. Add the eggs, then the corn meal, and more milk if necessary to make the batter thin enough to pour. Bake in greased, hot waffle irons. Serve piping hot.

Potato Griddle Scones

2 c. flour
1/2 t. salt
4 t. baking powder
2 T. shortening
1 egg, beaten
About 1 c. milk
3/4 c. cold mashed potatoes

Scones Sift flour, salt, and baking powder together. Rub in the shortening lightly, add the potatoes and mix to a soft dough with the egg and milk. Roll out about 3/4" thick, cut into three-cornered cakes and cook on hot, well greased griddle.

French Pancakes

1 c. flour
2 t. baking powder
1/2 t. salt
2 eggs, beaten
1 c. milk
Fruit preserves
Powdered sugar

Add eggs and milk to sifted flour, salt and baking powder. Beat well, being careful that there are no lumps. Melt a teaspoon of butter in a skillet. When pan is hot enough, pour in enough batter to just cover the bottom. Cook till golden brown, turn. Spread with fruit, roll up and sprinkle with powdered sugar just before serving.

Quick Coffee Cake

1 pint flour
1/2 t. salt
3 t. baking powder
1/2 t. cinnamon
1 egg
1/2 c. milk
3 T. lard, melted
1/2 c. sugar
More cinnamon

Sift together, twice, the flour, salt, baking powder and cinnamon. Beat egg well, stir in milk and add to the flour mixture. Mix to a soft dough. Add melted lard; spread in a shallow greased pan, sprinkle with sugar and some more cinnamon and bake in a moderate oven till done. Serve hot with butter.

Griddle Cakes

1 pint flour
1 c. milk
1 T. baking powder
1/2 t. sugar
1/2 t. salt

Sift together well the dry ingredients. Add milk to make into a soft batter; bake immediately on a hot griddle. Should be 1/8" thick when baked. Serve smothered in butter and maple syrup. These are the best plain hot griddle cakes without eggs and are light, tender and healthful. Just dandy!

King Kong roared his way into movie theaters in 1932-33. He was the most famous monster of his time, and even today remains very impressive. And who could ever forget Fay Wray's screaming?

12

Beverages

He sipped the nectar from her lips
As under the moon they sat
He said, "I bet that nobody else
Ever drank from a mug like that!"

Not one flavor...*but many mingled flavors*

— a mellow richness that has brought this blend such fame as never before came to a coffee

"Of the good things we have tasted in our lives," says a noted writer on foods, "most of us recall one or two most vividly of all—certain dishes in which we encountered a blend of flavors so enticing—so masterly that we cannot forget them.

"Back of the keenest pleasures of the table whether in a sauce, in a salad or a cup of coffee, lies always the work of some talented person who has joined taste with taste as a composer joins note with note in working out his harmonies."

Countless men and women who understand the fine points of good living have long set high value on this art of blending—and perhaps in coffee most of all.

With hundreds of kinds and grades of coffees brought from distant countries, with almost infinite shades of natural flavor to choose from, these Americans have been pleased with none of them.

Fame seldom equalled in the history of food has today come to one special mingling of flavors—to a blend of coffees perfected years ago in the South.

A southerner with an inborn genius for flavor, living in a land of critical tastes, Joel Cheek, down in old Tennessee created a blend which is today changing the habits of a nation.

Chosen by the most critical men and women of America

It was a particular touch of richness, a shade of difference in Joel Cheek's blend that first won it the approval of the great families of Dixie. Long ago it became the favorite of the cities of the South.

Today throughout the whole United States this same blend is pleasing more people than any other coffee ever offered for sale. Maxwell House has swiftly become by far the largest selling coffee in all America—the first choice of a long list of our notable cities.

In the full-bodied goodness and rich aroma of this blend your family will find a new contentment at breakfast and at dinner. That same shade of mellow difference which has delighted the most critical men and women of the country is now offered to you. Your grocer has Maxwell House Coffee in sealed blue tins. Cheek-Neal Coffee Company, Nashville, Houston, Jacksonville, Richmond, New York, Los Angeles.

Served for years to the notables of old Dixie at the Maxwell House in Nashville, the same of Joel Cheek's blend was soon carried through the whole South

"Good to the last drop"

MAXWELL HOUSE COFFEE

It is pleasing more people than any other coffee ever offered for sale

Coffee Preparation

There are many different ways to prepare coffee. It seems that making coffee is parallel to making potato salad: everyone has his or her own particular style. Here are a few detailed methods that agree on at least two basic rules of making fine coffee: the pot must be absolutely clean **and** always start with fresh, cold water.

Coffee

Making good coffee is an art easily acquired. Many a housewife has it, but her methods are various and the results are not always assured. The preservation of the aroma, flavor and quality of the coffee from the time of purchase until the time it is used depends upon several precautions:

1. Keep the coffee in a tight container that won't let in any light.
2. Do not expose it to the air by allowing it to remain uncovered.
3. Place the container where it will not be exposed to moisture.
4. See that the container is kept away from heat.
5. If you buy whole-bean coffee, grind it only in the quantity needed at the time of making.

All of these rules have to do with the retention of the flavor and aroma. While coffee in the bean loses both slowly, there are a number of ways in which carelessness will permit a rapid loss.

The most delicious results are obtained by using fresh roasted coffee, freshly ground, through which water of a temperature just below the boiling point is dripped for not more than two minutes. The rules to be followed to attain this most desired result are not hard to remember:

1. See that the coffee is not ground too coarse.
2. Allow at least a tablespoonful of ground coffee to a cup of water. The exact proportion depends upon the kind of coffee used and can be determined only by individual taste. In measuring the water always allow an extra cup of water to take care of evaporation.
3. Be sure the water boils; then pour it over the freshly ground coffee. By pouring at the boiling point, the water in contact with the coffee falls to just the temperature needed to extract the greatest amount of flavor and aroma.
4. Serve at once. Letting coffee cool ruins it. If there must be a delay in serving, keep the coffee piping hot, but do not let it boil.
5. Do not use the coffee grounds a second time.
6. Scour the coffee pot. Remnants of the old grounds will weaken the freshly ground coffee.

Coffee Preparation

Measuring: There is no set rule for the proper proportions of coffee and water. This will vary with the kind of coffee used, the way it is ground and the method of brewing, and above all, with individual taste. But once you have found the right proportion -- that is, the proportion best suited to your use -- stick to it! Don't guess. Measure carefully, both water and coffee. Remember that in brewing, the coffee grounds absorb a certain amount of the water in the pot. Therefore, to make five cups of coffee, use, say 5 1/2 cupfuls of water and in the same proportion when larger or smaller quantities are made.

Extracting Flavor: Chemists have analyzed the coffee bean and told us that its delicious taste is due to certain aromatic oils. This aromatic element is extracted most efficiently only by fresh boiling water. The practice of soaking the grounds in cold water, therefore, is to be condemned. It is a mistake also to let the water and the grounds boil together after the real coffee flavor is once extracted. This extraction takes place very quickly, especially when the coffee is ground fine. The coarser the granulation, the longer it is necessary to let the grounds remain in contact with the boiling water. Remember that flavor, the only flavor worth having, is extracted by the short contact of boiling water and coffee grounds, and that after this flavor is extracted, the coffee grounds become valueless dregs.

Use Once: Although the above rules are absolutely fundamental to good coffee making, their importance is so little appreciated that in some households the lifeless grounds from the breakfast coffee are left in the pot and resteeped for the next meal, with the addition of a small quantity of fresh coffee. Used coffee grounds are of no more value in coffee making than ashes are in kindling a fire.

Serve Immediately: After the coffee is brewed, the true coffee flavor, now extracted from the bean, should be guarded carefully. When the brewed liquid is left on the fire or overheated, this flavor is cooked away, and the whole character of the beverage is changed. It is just as fatal to let the brew grow cold. If possible, coffee should be served as soon as it is made. If service is delayed, it should be kept hot, but not overheated. For this purpose careful cooks prefer a double boiler over a slow fire. The cups should be warmed beforehand, and the same is true of a serving pot, if one is used. Brewed coffee, once injured by cooling, cannot be restored by reheating.

Scour the Pot: Unsatisfactory results in coffee brewing can frequently be traced to a lack of care in keeping utensils clean. The fact that the coffee pot is used only for coffee making is no excuse for setting it away with a hasty rinse. Coffee making utensils should be cleansed after each using with scrupulous care. If a percolator is used, pay special attention to the small tube through which the hot water rises to spray over the grounds. This should be scrubbed with the wire-handled brush that comes for that purpose.

Filter Bags: In cleansing drip or filter bags, use cool water. Hot water "cooks in" the coffee stains. After the bag is rinsed, keep it submerged in cool water until time to use it again. Never let it dry. This treatment protects the cloth from the germs in the air which cause souring. New filter bags should be washed before using to remove the starch or sizing.

Drip Coffee

The principle behind this method is the quick contact of water at the boiling point with the coffee, ground as fine as it is practical to use it. The filtering medium may be cloth or paper, or perforated chinaware or metal. The fineness of the grind should be regulated by the nature of the filtering medium, the grains being large enough not to slip through the perforations. The amount of ground coffee to use may vary from a heaping teaspoonful to a rounded tablespoonful for each cup of coffee desired, depending upon the granulation, the kind of apparatus used and the individual tastes. A general rule is the finer the grain, the smaller the amount of dry coffee required. The most satisfactory grind for a cloth drip bag has the consistency of coarse corn meal and shows a slight grit when rubbed between the thumb and finger. Unbleached muslin makes the best bag for this granulation. For dripping coffee reduced to a powder, as fine as flour or confectioner's sugar, use a bag of Canton flannel with the fuzzy side in. Powdered coffee, however, requires careful manipulation and cannot be recommended for everyday household use.

Put the ground coffee in the bag or sieve. Bring fresh water to a boil and pour it through the coffee at a steady, gradual rate of flow. If a cloth drip bag is used, with a very finely ground coffee, one pouring should be enough. No special pot or device is necessary. The liquid coffee may be dripped into any handy vessel or directly into the cups. Dripping into the coffee cups, however, is not to be recommended unless the dripper is moved from cup to cup so that no one cup will get more than its share of the first flow, which is the strongest and best.

The brew is complete when it drips from the grounds, and further cooking or "heating up" injures the quality. Therefore, since it is not necessary to put the brew over the fire, it is possible to make use of the hygienic advantages of a glassware, porcelain or earthenware pot.

Steeped Coffee

For steeping use a medium grind. The recipe is a rounded tablespoonful for each cup of coffee desired or -- as some cooks prefer to remember it -- a tablespoonful for each cup and "one for the pot." Put the dry coffee in the pot and pour over it fresh water briskly boiling. Steep for 5 minutes or longer, according to taste, over a low fire. Do not boil. Settle with a dash of cold water or strain through muslin or cheesecloth and serve at once.

Percolated Coffee

Use a rounded tablespoonful of medium-fine ground coffee to each cupful of water. The water may be poured into the percolator cold or at the boiling point. In the latter case, percolation begins at once. Let the water percolate over the grounds for 5 or 10 minutes, depending upon the intensity of the heat and the flavor desired.

Helen's Take-Forever Coffee

Put 6 cups of water on to boil in a tea kettle. Meanwhile, break an egg into a cup, crunch up the shell and toss that in too. Add about 1/4 c. water to the egg and beat it all up with a fork. Put about 4 T. freshly ground coffee into the coffeepot. Pour about 1/4 of the egg mixture and shell over the coffee and slosh it around. (Put the rest of the egg in the icebox for use later.) When water comes to a boil, gently pour it over the coffee in the pot. Put the pot on very low heat, and slowly, slowly bring it just to the point of boiling. (This seems to take forever...especially since it smells so good!) Then remove the pot from the heat, pour in about 1/4 c. very cold water and let it sit for about 5 minutes to settle the grounds. Pour through a fine sieve. Serve with cream and/or sugar. (Helen's guests would get pretty disgusted having to wait so long for the coffee, but it was worth it after all.)

Boiled Coffee

Use 2 T. coffee to 3 c. water. Grind the coffee moderately fine, add half the white of an egg to it and put into a perfectly clean coffeepot. Add enough cold water to moisten the coffee, then pour the measured water over. Cover the pot closely and boil ten minutes. Then pour in half a cup of cold water, draw the pot to the side of the range and allow it to stand five minutes to settle before serving. Never let the coffee boil after the cold water has been added.

Filtered Coffee

Use 1 T. of coffee to each cup of water. Have the coffee finely ground, the coffeepot hot and the water freshly boiling. Put the coffee into the strainer or upper part of the pot, measure the water and pour it slowly over the coffee. When it has filtered through, pour it again over the grounds, keeping the pot where the water will remain at the boiling point but not actually boil during the process. The pot may stand in a vessel of boiling water during the filtering process if desired.

After-Dinner Coffee

Make according to rule for Filtered Coffee, using twice the quantity of coffee to each cup of water. Serve in very small cups.

Cafe au Lait

Use 1 T. coffee to each cup of water. Grind the coffee finely, and prepare as in Filtered Coffee, using only half the quantity of water. When filtered twice, pour off the coffee and add an equal amount of freshly scalded milk.

Iced Coffee In Perfection

1 pint cold good coffee
1/4 t. cinnamon
1 pint milk
Whipped cream
Cracked Ice

Have both coffee and milk chilled; mix well, add cracked ice. Just before serving, put the whipped cream on top of the glass and dust over with cinnamon. This is very good on hot summer days.

Hot Chocolate

2 sq. chocolate
2 t. sugar
3 c. milk
Whipped cream
4 T. cold water
1 t. vanilla

Put chocolate into a sauce- pan or in the top of the double boiler with water and sugar. Cook over gentle heat till the chocolate is melted. Add milk gradually and bring to the boiling point. Beat till foamy, flavor with vanilla, and serve with a spoonful of whipped cream on top.

Hot Chocolate

Heat to the boiling point 1 cup of milk. Mix together 1 teaspoon cocoa and 1 teaspoon sugar and add to the milk. Stir until well dissolved. This makes one cup. Half water may be used.

Chocolate Cream Nectar

2 sq. chocolate
1/2 c. brewed coffee
3 c. water
1 c. sugar
1 t. vanilla
Whipped cream

Melt chocolate in saucepan over low heat. Add coffee and cook 2 minutes, stirring constantly. Add sugar and water and cook 5 minutes. Chill, add vanilla. Put about a tablespoon whipped cream into glasses, pour in chocolate. Be sure beverage is thoroughly chilled before serving.

Cocoa

2 T. cocoa
2 T. sugar
1 pint boiling water
1 pint boiling milk
Whipped cream

Put cocoa and sugar in a saucepan. Add 1/2 c. of the boiling water and cook, stirring constantly, for 5 minutes. Add rest of water and the milk and cook 5 minutes more. Serve with whipped cream.

Claret Punch

2/3 c. water
1 pt. claret
Juice of 2 lemons
Cracked ice
1 qt. water
2 sprigs mint
1 sliced orange
A few fresh strawberries

Dissolve the sugar in the water. Add the claret, lemon juice, ice and mint. Crush the mint a little to release the fragrance. Slice the orange thin and add with the strawberries just before serving.

Grape Juice

Grapes
Sugar

Pick grapes from stalks. Crush and place over a slow fire till the juice runs freely. Strain through a fine cloth or jelly bag, squeezing out all the juice. Measure. (For each quart of juice, use 1 1/2 c. sugar.) Scald juice, add sugar, boil 5 minutes after the sugar is melted. Bottle and seal.

Mint Cordial

1 lg. bunch mint
Juice of 2 lemons
1 lb. sugar
1 pt. water
Juice of 1 orange
1 c. pineapple juice

Pick off mint leaves, crush thoroughly, add lemon juice and stand aside for one hour. Boil the water and sugar to a syrup, pour over the mint and lemon. Cool and strain. Add orange and pineapple juices and serve with a sprig of fresh mint in each glass. Serve ice cold.

1939: "Gone With The Wind", the all-American classic film, kept movie patrons in their seats for a full 220 minutes. But who could resist Vivian Leigh and Clark Gable? Or Leslie Howard and Olivia de Havilland? The Technicolor was unusually impressive in this enormously successful film.

Mulled Cider

1 qt. cider
1/2 t. whole allspice
2" stick cinnamon
3 eggs, well beaten

Boil together the cider and spices for 3 minutes. Add juice carefully to the eggs, beating while adding. Strain and serve very hot.

Raspberry Vinegar

4 qts. raspberries
2 qts. cider vinegar
Sugar

Crush 2 qts. of raspberries, pour vinegar over them. Let stand 2 days. Strain, and pour the juice over the other 2 qts. berries. Let stand for another 2 days. Strain and measure. Add one pound of sugar for each pint. Boil five minutes; skim, bottle and seal. Use two T. to a tumbler of water.

Blackberry Cordial

1 qt. blackberry juice
1 lb. sugar
1 t. grd. clove
2 t. nutmeg
2 t. cinnamon
2 t. allspice
1 pt. brandy

Crush enough blackberries to give a qt. of juice. Put in a porcelain saucepan with the sugar. Tie the spices up in a bag, add to pan and cook 15 minutes after it boils. Skim and cover closely till cold. Strain, add the brandy, and bottle and seal. This will keep for years.

Lime Punch

8 cubes sugar
Juice of 2 oranges
Juice of 2 limes
1 1/2 c. water
Cracked ice
Slice of pineapple
2 crystallized cherries

Rub the cubes of sugar over the rind of the oranges and limes. Then put the sugar in a bowl and pour the lime and orange juices over it. Add the water, and serve when the sugar is melted; chilling with plenty of cracked ice. Put in the pineapple and cherries at the moment of serving. Makes two servings.

The murals we see even today in some post offices were painted by artists as a part of the 1935 Federal Arts Project.

Making Tea

Scald an earthenware or china teapot; put in 1 t. tea and pour on 2 c. of boiling water. Let stand on back of range or in a warm place 5 minutes. Strain and serve immediately with or without sugar and milk. Avoid a second steeping of leaves with the addition of a few fresh ones. If this is done, so large an amount of tannin is extracted that various ills are apt to follow.

Harvest Switchel

2 c. sugar
1 c. molasses
1/4 c. cider vinegar
1 t. ginger
1 gal. water

Mix sugar, molasses, vinegar and ginger in 1 qt. water; heat until dissolved. Add 3 more qts. water and chill. Serve cold! Switchel is especially thirst-quenching, so be sure to have plenty ready when it's haying time and the men are hot and sweaty.

Raspberry Shrub

1 qt. red raspberries
1 qt. water
3/4 c. sugar
Juice of 2 lemons

Put berries in a large bowl and mash to a pulp. Boil water, add sugar and lemon juice and pour over berries. When cool, press through a colander. Chill and serve over ice.

Cherry Shrub

1 qt. ripe cherries
1 qt. water
1 lb. sugar
Juice of 1 lemon

Stone cherries and mash through a colander. Boil water and sugar, add to cherries. Add lemon juice, stir well and chill. Serve partly frozen or with shaved ice. In hot weather, this will really cool you off!

Raspberry Vinegar

1 qt. wine vinegar
6 qt. red raspberries
Sugar

Pour vinegar over 2 qt. berries, let stand over- night. Strain through a jelly bag onto 2 more qts. berries. Next morning repeat this. Then to each pint liquid add 3/4 lb. sugar and boil all for 20 minutes. Bottle when cold. To serve, mix 2 T. to a glass of water.

1935: *An interesting coincidence: just 2 years after the lifting of prohibition, Alcoholics Anonymous was founded.*

Best Ever Lemonade

4 lemons
1 c. sugar
1 qt. water

Peel lemons and put rinds into a bowl. Cover with sugar and let stand 1/2 hour. Boil water, pour over lemons and sugar. When cool, take out rinds. Squeeze lemons, strain and add to sugar mixture. Chill and serve ice cold. Tastes better when sipped while sitting in a rocking chair on the porch!

Lemonade Syrup

2 T. lemon rind, grated
2 c. lemon juice (from
    about 8 lemons)
2 c. sugar
1 1/2 c. water

Mix together rind, juice and sugar. Stir until sugar is dissolved. Add the water, cover tightly and keep in the refrigerator. To serve, put 1/2 c. syrup in a large glass with ice, fill with water. Keep this syrup on hand all summer for a quick cold drink.

Dandelion Wine

1 qt. dandelion blossoms
1 gal. water
1 lemon, sliced
2 1/2 lbs. sugar
2 T. good yeast

Put all in a kettle, except yeast, and boil five minutes. Pour into a jar. When cold, add yeast. Keep in a warm place 3 days until it ferments, then strain and bottle - cork tightly.

Raisin Wine

2 lbs. raisins
1 lb. sugar
1 sliced lemon
2 gal. boiling water

Seed and chop raisins fine. Put into a large crock with sugar and lemon. Pour boiling water in. Stir daily for 6-8 days. Then strain and bottle and put in a cool place for 10 days and it will be ready.

1933: Prohibition was finally repealed on April 7th; it had gone into effect in 1920 with the ratification of the 18th Amendment. The legalization of beer cheered up a lot of folks, and Roosevelt's campaign song, "Happy Days are Here Again!" was on the lips of the nation.

Elderberry Blossom Wine

1 gal. boiling water
1 qt. elder blossoms
3 lbs. sugar
1 lemon, thinly sliced
1 T. good yeast

Put blossoms in a large kettle and pour water over them. Let stand 1 hour. Strain, add sugar to liquid, boil a little and skim. When lukewarm, add lemon and yeast. Let stand 24 hours, then strain and put into bottles or jugs, filling full until all impurities are worked out. Be sure to fill up jugs as fast as it works out and the wine will be a beautiful amber color. (In making this wine, be careful to keep all stems out, as they make the wine taste rank and give it a dark color.) Cork tightly.

Communion Wine

20 lbs. grapes,
    cleaned, no stems
6 qts. water
6 lbs. sugar

Put grapes and water in stone jars over the fire and cook until the skins and seeds separate from pulp. Strain through cheese cloth and return to jars; add sugar, and mix thoroughly with a wooden spoon. Use absolutely no tin, iron or even silver about the wine. Strain again through fresh cheese cloth and put in jars over the fire. Do not boil hard, but allow it to heat gradually until it begins to simmer. Bottle at once.

A Cranberry Drink

1/2 pt. cranberries
1/2 gal. water
1/2 lemon, peeled
1 oz. oatmeal
A little sugar
2 glasses wine

Put cranberries over the fire to boil. In another kettle, boil water, lemon and oatmeal for 10-15 minutes. Add cranberries and sugar - just enough so as not to take away the acid of the fruit. Add wine. Boil for 20 minutes, strain and serve cold.

Blackberry Wine

1 gal. black berries
1 qt. boiling water
2 lbs. sugar

Bruise berries, add boiling water. Let stand 24 hours, stirring occasionally. Strain off the liquor and put into a cask. Add sugar; cork tight and let stand till next October, when it will be ready for use. It may be bottled.

Cottage Beer

1 peck good wheat bran
3 handsful hops
2 qts. molasses
2 T. yeast
10 gal. water

Put wheat bran and hops into water, and boil until bran and hops sink to the bottom. Strain through a thin cloth into a cooler. When it is about lukewarm, add molasses. As soon as molasses is dissolved, pour all into a 10-gallon cask and add yeast. When fermentation is over with, cork up the cask and it will be ready in 4-5 days.

Ginger Beer

6 oz. bruised ginger
3 qts. water
5 lbs. loaf sugar
1/4 lb. honey
A gill of lemon juice
17 qts. water
2 drachms essence of lemon
    (about 2 t.)
1 whole egg

Put ginger and 3 qts. water into a very large kettle and boil for 30 minutes. Add sugar, honey, lemon juice and 17 qts more water. Strain through a cloth and when it is cold add essence of lemon and egg. Let stand for 3-4 days before bottling.

Spruce Beer

2 oz. hops
1/2 gal. water
8 gal. warm water
1 gal. molasses
4 oz. essence of spruce   in
1 pt. water
1/4 pt. yeast
Molasses

Put hops and water in a kettle and boil for 30 minutes. Strain; add 8 gallons warm water, molasses and spruce essence. Put in a clean cask, shake all well together and add yeast. Let stand and work for 6-7 days, or less if the weather is warm. When drawn off, add 1 t. molasses to each bottle.

Due to the popularity of cars, and therefore people being able to travel farther from their homes, motels had been around since 1925. They were called bungalows, and pretty much consisted of a little wooden shack with a bed in it. There was outdoor plumbing and that was about it. But at least you didn't have to drag a tent along.

Recipes to Remember

Soups

To "pour oil on the troubled waters"
Makes many, ah! many a dupe;
For the peace of both men and nations
There never was aught like soup.

There's a glow of sunshine in this invigorating
Tomato Soup!

The bright color tempts and invites! The very first taste refreshes. And there's tonic and invigoration in every spoonful of this famous Tomato Soup!

In our spotless kitchens, the luscious tomatoes are washed five times in running water, cooked, and then strained through mesh as fine as pin points, retaining all the rich tomato goodness — the appetizing juices and nourishing tomato "meat" in a smooth puree.

Country butter, fresh herbs and dainty seasoning are blended in and the soup is cooked in tureens of pure nickel to yield the finest flavor.

A real treat! A soup that appeals to the whole family! Splendid for the children! Extra nourishing served as Cream of Tomato Soup (see directions on label).

21 kinds
12 cents a can

Two cans in one!
Remember that Campbell's is CONDENSED. The right amount of water added by you DOUBLES the quantity of soup you enjoy. This means real economy as well as splendid quality.

Woman's Home Companion June 1926

Chicken Stock

Bones and skin from
  1-2 chickens
4-8 qts. water
1/2-1 onion, chopped
salt and pepper
1 garlic clove

Put the chicken carcass in a large kettle.
Cover with water. Add the onion, bay leaf,
garlic, salt and pepper. Bring to a boil, then
simmer slowly on the back of the range for
several hours. Strain through colander, pick
meat from bones and add to stock. Cool,
skim fat off top. (Every time we had chicken
for supper, whether it was roasted or fried,
Mom would make "soup stock" to use for
gravy, soup and in hot dishes.)

Beef Stock

Beef stock can be made in the same way as Chicken Stock, by using a soup
bone or the bones from a roast in place of the chicken bones.

Turkey Soup

1 turkey carcass
Water to cover
1 med. onion
1 stalk celery
1/2 t. extract of beef
2 T. rice
Salt & pepper to taste

Break carcass into pieces; remove any
stuffing. Cover with water, add onion and
simmer two hours. Meanwhile, cook rice in
salted water. Remove turkey bones and
strain. Add extract of beef and rice. Bring to
the boiling point, season and serve with
croutons of fried bread.

Croutons

Cut stale, crustless bread into 1/2" cubes and fry until golden in hot fat. Or
cut buttered bread into cubes and toast in a hot oven. Either way, drop into
soup just before serving, or pass around the table.

Chicken Soup

Chicken stock
  Asst'd vegetables:
    Carrots, Celery,
    Celery leaves,
    Green beans,
    Tomatoes, Onion,
    Cabbage (optional)
Rice or noodles
Parsley
Salt & pepper

The amount of vegetables to use depends
upon how much soup you need to make.
Pare and slice all vegetables. Add to soup
stock and simmer a few hours or until
vegetables are done. Taste and correct
seasoning, add parsley. If you are making
the soup with rice, add it about 1/2 hour
before serving. If you are making noodle
soup, add about 1/4 hour before serving.

Poor Man's Soup

1 soup bone
1 c. dry pea beans
2 c. tomatoes (1 qt.)
1 c. chopped celery
1 c. diced potatoes
1/2 c. raw rice
1/3 lb. ground beef
1/3 c. chopped onion
Salt and pepper
1/8 t. basil

Pick over beans and soak overnight. Simmer soup bone in 8 qts. water for several hours. Add beans, simmer 45 minutes. Meanwhile, fry beef and onion. Add to soup along with remaining ingredients and simmer for one hour.

Vegetable Soup

4 T. butter
1/2 c. turnips, diced
1/2 c. carrots, chopped
1/2 c. celery, cut up
1 small onion, chopped
1 1/2 c. raw
    potatoes, diced
1 qt. water or broth
1 T. salt
Pepper to taste
1-2 T. ketchup

Melt butter in a large kettle and add vegetables (except potatoes). Fry until vegetables are a nice brown. Put in potatoes and water; cover and simmer slowly for about 2 hours. Add salt, pepper and ketchup just before serving. The secret to good soup is to simmer very slowly, never allowing it to boil.

Tomato Bisque

6 fresh tomatoes
1 small onion
1 1/2 pts. water
1 bay leaf
2 cloves
1 sprig parsley
2 T. butter
2 T. flour
1/2 t. baking soda
1 T. hot water
Salt & pepper to taste
1 pt. milk, scalded

Slice tomatoes and put them in a kettle with the onion, water, bay leaf, cloves and parsley. When tender, pass all through a sieve, rubbing the pulp through too. Blend butter and flour in a pan till smooth - do not brown! Add hot tomato liquid and stir till boiling. Season to taste. After cooking 5 minutes, add the soda in water. (This neutralizes the acid of the tomatoes.) Just before serving, add the hot milk.

"Let onion atoms lurk within the bowl,
And, half suspected, animate the whole."
                                        -Sidney Smith

Ma's Pea Soup

1 to 1 1/2 lbs. peas
1 ham bone
3 potatoes, halved
3 carrots, sliced
1 onion, chopped
Salt & pepper to taste

Wash and pick over peas to remove any little stones. Put in a large kettle, cover with water and simmer a few hours. Meanwhile, simmer ham bone covered with water, separately from the peas. When peas are soft, strain them. Put back into kettle, add ham picked from the bone, ham juice and remaining ingredients. Peas will mush up and turn into a puree as the soup finished cooking. Simmer gently until potatoes are done.

Cream of Oyster Soup

1 pt. oysters
1 qt. milk, scalded
1 T. butter
1 T. flour
Salt & pepper
1/2 c. whipped cream

Drain liquid from oysters and add an equal amount of water to it. Heat liquids slowly, skim well. Meanwhile chop oysters; add to liquid and cook 3 minutes. Cream butter and flour, add to scalded milk to thicken. Add milk mixture and seasonings. Put in the cream at the last minute before serving.

Clam Chowder

1 1/2 dz. clams
2 strips bacon, diced
1 onion, sliced
1 c. water
3 lg. potatoes, diced
1 qt. milk
2 T. butter
2 T. flour
Sat & pepper
8 crackers
1 t. parsley

Drain clams and chop fine; save liquid. Fry out the bacon, fry onion in fat. Add clam liquid, water and potatoes. Cook until tender; season, and add the clams and milk. Cook 10 minutes more, then thicken with butter and flour creamed together. Pour chowder over the crackers and sprinkle with parsley. This tastes really good, especially on a cold winter night.

Johnny Weismuller became Tarzan in 1932, Jane being played by Maureen O'Sullivan. Independent companies released other "Tarzan" features starring Buster Crabbe in 1933, Herman Brix in 1935, and Glenn Morris in 1938.

Tomato Soup

1 qt. tomatoes
3 small onions, chopped
1 pt. water
Salt & pepper, to taste
Butter the size
    of a walnut
A pinch of baking soda
Soda crackers

Put tomatoes, onions and water in a kettle and stew for about an hour. Remove from stove and strain through a sieve. Put back into kettle and add salt and pepper, butter, soda and milk. Bring to a boil. Crumble in soda crackers and serve. You could simply open a can of Campbell's, but this is really better!

Clam Broth

6 lg. clams in shell
1 1/2 c. water
1/2 t. butter
Salt & pepper

Scrub shells well; put them in a pan with 1 c. of the water. Cook till shells open; remove clams, chop them and return them to pan with the water. Cook 10 minutes, strain and add remaining water if necessary to reduce the strength of the broth. Season, serve.

Mutton Broth

2 lbs. neck of mutton
2 qts. cold water
1 t. salt
1 small turnip, diced
1 carrot, diced
1 onion, diced
2 T. barley
Salt & pepper to taste
1 t. parsley

Wipe off meat with a damp cloth. Cut meat into small pieces and put into a sauce- pan with water. Let it come slowly to a boil and then add the salt, which causes any scum to rise. Simmer for one hour, skimming the scum occasionally. Add vegetables and barley and cook till the vegetables are very tender. Season to taste; add parsley just before serving.

Ma's Turkey Soup

1 turkey carcass,
    skin & giblets
1 lg. onion, sliced
3-4 carrots, sliced
3-4 stalks celery, with
    leaves, chopped
Another onion, sliced
1 T. parsley
Salt & pepper to taste
A few handfuls
    of egg noodles

Put turkey bones, skin and giblets in a large pot and cover with water. Add onion, bring to a boil and simmer for several hours. Strain. Skim off fat and pick meat from bones. Put stock and meat back into the pot and add remaining ingredients. Simmer until vegetables are done. Add noodles the last 10 minutes before serving. A batch of popovers served with the soup makes it seem less "ordinary."

Chicken Gumbo

1 small chicken
2 qts. boiling water
1 c. corn
6 tomatoes, chopped
24 okra pods
Fat for frying
2 T. rice
Salt & pepper to taste

Cut up chicken and fry in fat. Cover and cook until tender. Meanwhile, fry corn, tomatoes and okra to a light brown in pan drippings from chicken. Remove meat from bones and chop fine. (Use bones and skin to make stock.) Place meat in kettle with water and simmer. Add all ingredients to stewing juices and simmer gently for an hour.

Vegetable Soup

3 onions, chopped
3 turnips, diced
2 carrots, sliced
4 potatoes, halved
2 T. butter
1 t. powdered sugar
2 qts. stock

Put vegetables into a stew pot with butter and sugar; fry gently for about 10 minutes. Don't let it burn. Then add the stock. Let it come to a boil and simmer gently until the vegetables are nice and tender, about 1/2 hour or so. You might want to add some noodles or rice to the soup. Good with corn bread.

Cream of Celery Soup

5 pts. water
3 c. celery, chopped fine
1 T. butter
1 T. flour
1 c. milk
Celery salt or extract
Salt & pepper to taste
1 c. milk, scalded

Cook celery in water until it's very tender; drain. Melt butter in saucepan and stir in flour; slowly add milk and cook until thick. Rub celery through a sieve, add to milk mixture. Add celery salt or extract and salt and pepper. Simmer 10 minutes. Add the hot milk just before serving for a rich, delicious soup.

1931: *The Empire State Building was opened, perhaps an inspiration for the 1933 release of "King Kong."*

1936: *Mickey Mouse was 8 years old that year, when he was joined on the big screen by his pal, Donald Duck.*

Oxtail Soup

3 T. drippings
2 oxtails
1 lg. onion, diced
1 carrot, diced
2 qts. cold water
2 stalks celery
2 sprigs parsley
1 bay leaf
2 T. pearly barley
1 T. flour in 2 T. water
Salt & pepper, or cayenne

Melt fat; fry oxtails (or beef tails), onion and carrot until brown; add water or stock. Tie the celery, parsley and bay leaf together (this is called a bouquet garni;) add to soup. Bring to a boil, add barley and simmer 4 hours. Remove large bones and bouquet garni; thicken soup with flour paste. Season rather highly and serve.

Peanut Soup

4 c. boiling water
1/2 lb. peanut butter
   OR
1/2 lb. ground peanuts
Salt to taste
Cream or canned milk

Boil peanut butter in water until thoroughly mixed; salt to taste. When ready to serve add a little cream or milk to each bowl. This is a very nourishing soup and children are especially fond of it.

Amber Soup

2 lb. soup bones
1 chicken
1 slice ham
1 gal. cold water
2 eggs, separated
1 onion
1 carrot
1/2 parsnip
1 stalk celery
3 cloves
Salt & pepper to taste
Caramel (see next recipe)

Boil the meats together for 4 hours. Fry onion in a little fat, add it and the other vegetables to the soup. Add cloves, season and simmer 1 hour longer. Strain into an earthen bowl, cool overnight. Remove fat; take out the jelly, avoiding the settlings. Mix in well- beaten egg whites and beaten egg yolks. Boil quickly for 1/2 minute, remove from heat. Skim off top, being careful not to stir soup. Pass through a jelly bag; it should be very clear. Reheat just before serving, adding 1 T. caramel to give it rich color and flavor.

Caramel

1 c. sugar
1 T. water
1 c. water
A pinch of salt

Put sugar and the 1 T. water into a porcelain kettle, cook and stir constantly till a bright brown color. Add water and salt, let boil a few more minutes. Cool, strain and bottle; cork tightly. Always ready for coloring soups.

Cream of Tomato Soup

1 qt. tomatoes
1/2 t. baking soda
1/4 c. butter
1/3 c. flour
1 qt. milk
Salt & pepper

Simmer tomatoes in a covered saucepan for about 15 minutes. Press through a strainer and add baking soda. In saucepan, melt butter, stir in flour and cook till thick. Slowly add milk. Remove from stove and slowly add the hot tomatoes, stirring constantly. Season and serve at once.

Bouillon

1 lb. beef from the round
1 pt. cold water
1 sprig parsley
1 stalk celery
1 t. salt
Pepper to taste
Caramel (pg. 34)

Chop beef into very small pieces. Put it in a saucepan with water, parsley and celery. Cook and stir with a wooden spoon until the meat is almost white. Remove from heat and let stand 30 minutes. Return to stove and quickly bring to a boil, add salt, pepper. Strain through a napkin, color with caramel and it is ready to serve.

Beef Broth

1 lb. lean beef, minced
1 qt. cold water
2 T. rice
Salt & pepper

Boil beef and rice in water about 1 hour. Strain, add salt and pepper to taste and serve hot.

White Soup

2 qts. meat broth
3 eggs, beaten
2 c. milk
2 T. flour
Salt & pepper

Bring meat broth to boiling point. Beat together the well-beaten eggs, milk and flour. Pour egg mixture gradually through a sieve into the boiling soup. Season to taste and serve.

Vegetable Soup

1 soup bone
6 potatoes, diced
1/2 head cabbage
2 onions, chopped fine
2 stalks celery, chopped
1/2 c. rice
3 tomatoes

Make a nice stock with the soup bone by boiling it for 2 hours in about 2 qts. water. Remove bone, add the vegetables and rice and simmer until vegetables are tender. Season to taste with salt and pepper; serve very hot.

Beef Stew

2 T. fat
1 onion, chopped
1 1/2 lbs. stew meat, cubed
1 qt. water
4 potatoes, quartered
3 carrots, sliced
1 stalk celery
2-3 T. flour in
   1/2 c. water
Salt & pepper to taste
Caramel (pg. 34)

Melt fat in heavy pot, add onion and fry until light brown. Remove from pot; add meat and fry until well browned. Add water and onion; cover and simmer until meat is tender. About 1/2 hour before serving, add potatoes, carrots and celery. Just before serving, mix flour with 1/2 c. water and stir into stew. Add salt, pepper and caramel; stir to blend and serve hot.

Bean Soup

2 strips bacon
1 onion, sliced
1 c. navy beans
Water to cover
Salt & pepper to taste
Cream or evaporated milk

Chop up bacon and fry in a heavy pot. Add onion and cook until light brown. Add beans and carefully pour in water. Simmer gently until beans are soft, about 2 hours. Rub through a colander, or leave whole if you prefer. Season well; add a few spoonfuls of cream to each bowl and serve with toast squares. Some prefer corn bread.

Garden Soup

6 T. fat
4 stalks celery
2 lg. onions
3 cloves garlic,
   minced fine
1 green pepper
2 lbs. ground beef
6 tomatoes
2 c. fresh cooked
   kidney beans
1 t. salt
1 T. honey
1 T. vinegar

Peel and chop vegetables. Melt fat in a large pot and fry celery, onion, garlic and pepper until browned. Add tomatoes, beans, salt, honey and vinegar. Simmer gently for an hour or two, stirring often to prevent scorching. If soup becomes too thick, add 1-2 cups hot water. Serve with soda crackers or fresh, hot rolls.

1931: *October 21, The George Washington Bridge was opened, connecting Manhattan to the New Jersey Palisades.*

October 30, 1931: *NBC was granted permission to operate an experimental television station.*

Meats

Beef, Pork, Lamb & Game

"Some hae meat and canna eat,
And some would eat that want it;
But we hae meat, and we can eat,
Sae let the Lord be thankit."
-Burns

S W I F T
A Food Service

Shopping for meat

There is a meat for every meal and a cut for every need

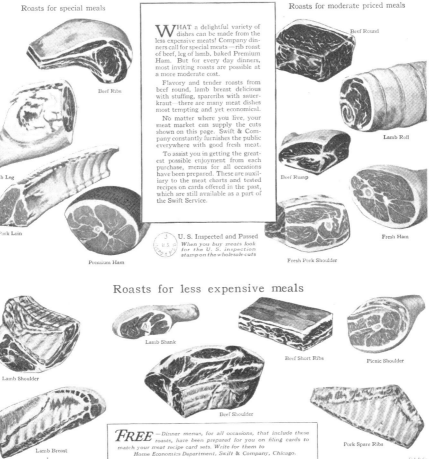

Roasts for special meals

Roasts for moderate priced meals

WHAT a delightful variety of dishes can be made from the less expensive meats! Company dinners call for special meats—rib roast of beef, leg of lamb, baked Premium Ham. But for every day dinners, most inviting roasts are possible at a more moderate cost.

Flavory and tender roasts from beef round, lamb breast delicious with stuffing, spareribs with sauerkraut—there are many meat dishes most tempting and yet economical.

No matter where you live, your meat market can supply the cuts shown on this page. Swift & Company constantly furnishes the public everywhere with good fresh meat.

To assist you in getting the greatest possible enjoyment from each purchase, menus for all occasions have been prepared. These are auxiliary to the meat charts and tested recipes on cards offered in the past, which are still available as a part of the Swift Service.

U. S. Inspected and Passed
When you buy meats look for the U. S. inspection stamp on the wholesale cuts

Beef Ribs

Lamb Leg

Pork Loin

Premium Ham

Beef Round

Lamb Roll

Beef Rump

Fresh Ham

Fresh Pork Shoulder

Roasts for less expensive meals

Lamb Shank

Beef Short Ribs

Picnic Shoulder

Lamb Shoulder

Beef Shoulder

Pork Spare Ribs

Lamb Breast

FREE — Dinner menus, for all occasions, that include these roasts, have been prepared for you on filing cards to match your meat recipe card sets. Write for them to Home Economics Department, Swift & Company, Chicago.

© S & Co.

Gillan's Liver Bologna

3 lbs. liver
8 lbs. potatoes, sliced
1/4 slab bacon
1/4 c. salt
2 1/2 c. graham flour
1/2 c. buttermilk
2 1/4 c. white flour

Make bags out of flour sacks. This recipe will fit into four 6 X 12" bags. Grind liver and potatoes, using a medium blade. Cut bacon into little pieces. Mix meats, potatoes and other ingredients in a very large bowl. When evenly combined, pack mixture into damp bags. Tie shut. Boil bags in water to cover, for two hours. Remove from water and cool. Store in refrigerator. To use, cut bag off meat, slice meat and serve.

This may have been one of the first take-along "mountain foods." Some deer hunters would take this out in the woods with them for food, as it was a complete meal - better than beef jerky!

Swedish Sausage

1 1/2 lb. beef
1 1/2 lb. pork
Potatoes
Salt & pepper
1-2 onions, chopped

Grind together the beef and pork. Grind an equal amount of raw potatoes. Add salt and pepper to taste and mix thoroughly. Put into casings; boil slowly for one hour. You can leave out the onions and it's still good.

Veal-Ham Pot Pie

3 c. veal, cubed
1. c. smoked ham,
    cooked and cubed
2 small onions
4 potatoes, sliced
1/2 c. carrots, chopped
1 c. celery, chopped
1 t. salt
1/2 t. pepper
3 whole cloves
2 T. fat
3 T. flour

2 recipes of
    Baking Powder Biscuits-
    one for pot pie,
    the other for passing
    (page 4)

Put veal in large kettle and cover with water. Cook slowly till it's tender. Add rest of ingredients except fat and flour. Simmer till vegetables are done. Drain, reserving liquid, and put mixture into a casserole. Measure liquid, add water to make 3 cups. Melt fat, stir in flour, and slowly add hot liquid. Stir and cook until thick, pour over meat mixture. Put baking powder biscuits on top so that they are just touching. Bake in hot oven until biscuits are browned. If you cut the biscuits with a doughnut cutter, the gravy bubbles up through centers and around the biscuits to make a nice top. Serve with the extra baking powder biscuits.

Dresses could be purchased for $1.49. If you wanted a dress with a jacket to match, you'd have to splurge: $2.98.

Uncle John's Navy Hash

Cold baked potatoes
Cold pot roast or
   whatever you have
Assorted leftover
   vegetables: carrots,
   cabbage, celery
1 onion, chopped
2 eggs, beaten
Soda crackers, crushed

This is a real good way to use up leftovers, and it tastes great, too. Cut potatoes, meat and vegetables into pieces. Fry meat and onion together until onion is cooked. Add potatoes and vegetables and fry till hot. Stir in beaten eggs to bind all together. Add crushed crackers. You might want to serve this with some ketchup, but, it's good and filling all by itself.

Country Pork Sausage

6 lbs. lean pork
3 lbs. fat pork
3 T. salt
2 T. black pepper
1/4 t. red pepper
4 T. sage, sifted

Put the pork through the meat grinder, add the seasonings and mix thoroughly. Grind again, so the meat may be nice and fine. Savory, mace, cloves and nutmeg may be added if you like.

Kaldomar (Swedish)

1 lb. beef
1/2 lb. pork
1/2 c. rice
Grated onion
Salt & pepper
A lg. cabbage

Soak rice in cold water for about an hour, drain. While rice is soaking, place a large head of cabbage in boiling water and let stand until the leaves are wilted and can be removed without breaking. Grind together beef and pork. Mix in rice, onion, salt and pepper. Wrap meat carefully in cabbage leaves, place close together in kettle, cover with cold water and boil slowly till done.

Grandpa Gus made his own radio, actually a crystal set. He had some sort of a metal bar which he wrapped with wire. There was a small, shiny rock (hence, "crystal" set) that was connected to the coil with a fine wire called a "cat's whisker." The whisker was moved around until the best spot was found for clear reception. Gus somehow hooked the whole thing up to a pair of headphones, and there! Radio! Sometimes he'd have to share the headphones with his wife, Signe, who wanted to listen at the same time - it was quite a comical sight. The guy in the neighborhood who could make the best crystal set was a regular hero, and a popular man, since he could save the folks the cost of buying a radio.

Lamb with Macaroni

2 c. macaroni, cooked
4 c. lamb, cooked, minced
1 1/2 c. tomato sauce
1 small onion, chopped
1/2 green pepper, chopped

Put 1 c. macaroni into a buttered baking dish. Add 2 c. lamb, another layer of macaroni and another layer of lamb. Mix the tomato sauce, onion and green pepper together. Pour evenly over layers. Sprinkle with crumbs and bake till heated through.

Beef or Veal Loaf

1 1/2 lbs. beef or veal
1 small piece salt pork
2 eggs
6 soda crackers
1/2 t. poultry seasoning
1 T. celery, chopped
1/2 t. salt
1/2 t. pepper
3/4 c. milk

Grind together beef or veal and salt pork. Put meat into a bowl and make a depression in the middle. Drop in whole eggs. Crush crackers fine, add to meat. Sprinkle on seasonings, pour in milk. Mix well together and put into loaf pan. Bake at 350 degrees for about an hour. Pour off fat after about 50 minutes. Leftovers are good made into sandwiches. But there usually aren't any leftovers.

Mock Quail

1 pork or veal loin
Stuffing
Flour
Salt & pepper
Butter
Water

Cut meat into pieces about 4" long. Make an incision sideways to create a cavity. Fill with you favorite stuffing and close with a toothpick. Roll in flour, season and bake; basting with butter and water. It isn't quail, but you may fool them.

Real Quail

6 or more quail
18 slices bacon
    or salt pork
1 T. butter
Stuffing, if desired

Draw and dry-pluck birds. Cover high exposed surfaces with bacon or salt pork and tie around bird. Melt butter in skillet, put in quail and bake in a hot oven for about 5 minutes. Reduce heat to about 350 degrees and bake another 15 minutes. If birds are stuffed, bake 20 minutes.

Radio broadcasts provided a wonderful, free variety show. People tuned in to hear such greats as Fibber McGee and Molly, Amos 'n' Andy, Charlie McCarthy and his ventriloquist Edgar Bergen (so who could see his lips move anyway?), Jack Benny and Mary Livingston, "The Goldberg's" show, Rudy Vallee and, of course, George Burns and Gracie Allen.

Veal Croquettes

1 c. white sauce
4 c. cooked veal, chopped
1 t. salt
1/2 t. pepper
2 t. lemon juice
Cracker crumbs

Make a white sauce: melt 2 T. butter, stir in 2 T. flour, salt and pepper. Slowly add 1 c. milk and stir till thick and smooth. Mix together sauce and other ingredients; let cool. When cool, mold into any shape and roll in cracker crumbs. Deep fry in hot lard. These are really good!

Veal Collops

Lean veal
1 t. salt
1/2 t. pepper
1/4 t. mace
1 egg, beaten well
Cracker crumbs

Cut meat into pieces the size of an oyster. Mix together spices - rub a little into each piece of meat. Dip in egg, then into cracker crumbs; fry. They both look and taste like oysters. If you don't have any veal, and you substitute oysters, they'll still taste like oysters.

Veal Cutlets

1 1/2 lbs. veal cutlets,
   cut thick
1 egg, beaten well
Cracker crumbs
Salt
Pepper

Season cutlets with salt and pepper. Dip into egg, then into crumbs, coating thoroughly. Shake off all loose crumbs. Fry in hot fat and cook the meat golden brown. Veal must always be thoroughly done. Serve with gravy or tomato sauce. These are wonderfully "sticky." The kids will love them and so will you.

Baked Lamb Chops

6 lg. potatoes
1 small onion,
Salt & pepper
Cold water
6 lamb chops

Slice potatoes and lay in a flat, open baking dish. Put the onion, salt and pepper on top. Cover with cold water, and put lamb chops on top of that, with a little more salt. Bake at 350 degrees for about 1 1/4 hours.

Hemlines were lower than they were in the 20's, and waistline styles returned, giving women a more sophisticated, sleeker look.

1931: *The first double-feature was introduced, creating even more hours of diversion at "the show."*

Stuffed Shoulder of Mutton

1 lg. mutton shoulder
1 c. bread crumbs
1 T. parsley, chopped
Grated rind of 1/2 lemon
1 T. fat
Salt & pepper
1 egg, beaten well

Remove the blade bone from the shoulder, or have the butcher do it. Mix together the crumbs, parsley, lemon rind, fat, salt, pepper and egg. Stuff the boned cavity, sew up the opening, and roast. Be sure to baste frequently with a little fat or the meat will be dry. Allow 15 minutes to the pound. Serve with gravy.

Mrs. T.'s Ham Loaf

1 lb. ham
1 lb. pork
1/2 green pepper
1 small onion
1 egg
Cracker crumbs
Salt & pepper
1 can tomato soup

Grind ham and pork together. Chop green pepper and onion. Add to meats. Add egg, crumbs and salt and pepper. Mix well and place in a loaf pan. Bake at 350 degrees for about an hour. Serve on a platter, and pour over a can of tomato soup heated up with a little water.

Southern Baked Ham

A 12-14 lb. ham
Water to cover
1 c. brown sugar
Cream or water
Cloves

Soak ham overnight in water. In the morning put it on to boil in the same water. Boil till tender. Remove from kettle, skin the ham. Make a paste of the brown sugar and cream or water, spread over ham, stick full of cloves. Bake about an hour.

Baked Smoked Ham

A 5-8 lb. ham
1 carrot, sliced
1 onion, peeled
1 small bay leaf
Prepared mustard
1/3 c. whole cloves
1 c. brown sugar
1 c. fine bread crumbs
Vinegar

Wipe ham with a damp cloth. Put in a large kettle, add carrot, onion and bay leaf and cover with water. Bring to a boil and simmer until tender. Let ham cool in water it was cooked in. Remove ham rind and score the fat with criss-crosses. Spread with mustard and stick cloves in score marks. Mix together sugar and crumbs with a little vinegar - press this in a thick layer all over the ham. Bake slowly to brown.

The Listerine Mouthwash people cautioned, "Who cares if your gown is beautiful? How's your breath today? Don't guess, use Listerine and be sure."

Ham Slice with Curried Fruit

1 slice ham, 1" thick
1/2 c. brown sugar
1 c. fine bread crumbs
3 T. Water
Salt & pepper
2 t. mustard

Trim fat off ham. Chop fat, mix with other ingredients. Wipe ham with a damp cloth. Put it into a baking pan and cover with the crumb mixture. Bake 1 hour at 375 degrees and baste 3-4 times. When ham is in the oven, make Curried Fruit.

Curried Fruit
Canned peaches, pears,
    and/or apricots
Sliced canned pineapple
1/2 c. butter, melted
1 c. brown sugar
1 T. curry powder

Drain fruits, and put as much as will fit into a deep baking dish. Mix butter with sugar and curry powder and pour over fruit. Bake in same oven as ham for 40 minutes. Serve from baking dish with ham.

Creamed Dried Beef

1/4 lb. dried beef
2 T. butter
1-2 T. flour
1 c. milk
Hot buttered toast

Pick meat in small pieces, brown in butter. Sprinkle on flour and stir. Slowly add milk; cook until slightly thickened. When it boils, pour it over a platter of toast and serve at once.

Swedish Rull Sylta

1 lg. veal flank
1 lb. mutton
1 lb. pork
2 onions, sliced
Salt & pepper
Allspice
Cloves

Cut mutton and pork in thin slices. Wash flank well and place on a cutting board. Put mutton and pork on flank. Lay onion slices on top and sprinkle with seasonings. Roll up tightly and sew together. Put into a kettle of boiling water and simmer 3 hours. Remove and place in a low earthen dish; put a plate on top of meat to weight it down. Put in ice box; let stand a day or two before using.

Pork Chops and Apples

4 pork chops
2 apples, cored
Brown sugar
Salt & pepper

Brown chops. Place 1/2 apple, cut crosswise, on each chop and fill with brown sugar. Bake in moderate oven for an hour. Season with salt and pepper. Easy.

1931: *The first sound picture, "Trader Horn," was filmed on location in Africa.*

Pork Chop Casserole

4 thick pork chops
2-3 tart apples
4 sweet potatoes, peeled
Salt & pepper
1/4 c. water

Wipe off chops, place in a deep covered casserole. Peel and slice apples, place on chops. Sprinkle with salt and pepper. Slice potatoes 1/2" thick and put on top of apples. Salt and pepper, add water. Cover tightly and bake 1 hour at 400 degrees. Uncover till browned on top. You can use regular white potatoes in place of sweet potatoes. This is a good one-dish meal. They don't seem to tire of it, either.

Ham Loaf

1 lb. fresh pork
1/2 lb. beef
1/2 lb. smoked ham
1/2 c. tomatoes
1/4 c. bread crumbs
1 egg, well beaten

Grind meats all together. Add a pinch of salt, a little pepper and the tomatoes, bread crumbs and egg. Form into a loaf and bake for about 45 minutes. Serve with tomato sauce: simmer 1/2 c. tomatoes, a few onion slices, 4-5 cloves and a little salt and pepper. Meanwhile, melt 1 T. butter, stir in 1 T. flour, and strain sauce into this. Cook until thickened.

Fried Sweetbreads

Sweetbreads
1-2 eggs, beaten
Cracker crumbs
Butter
Salt & pepper

Soak sweetbreads in cold water for 2 hours. Clean and parboil them for 15 minutes. Cook and slice, then dip in egg, then in cracker crumbs and fry in butter. Season to taste.

Stuffed Calf's Heart

1 calf's heart
3/4 c. bread crumbs
2 T.butter, melted
2 T. celery, chopped
2 T. onion, chopped
Salt & pepper
4 slices bacon
1/2 c. water or
    pineapple juice

Wash heart under running water. Cut out cords and veins and wipe dry. Mix bread crumbs, butter, celery, onion and seasonings. Fill heart cavity. Sew the opening shut. Dredge with flour and place in baking pan; put bacon on top of heart. Pour water or juice into pan and bake in a moderately hot oven, basting frequently. If you use a beef heart, double the stuffing recipe and leave out the pineapple juice. Cook at a lower temperature and for a longer time.

Liver Pudding

1 lb. liver
1 c. rice
1 onion, chopped
1/2 c. corn syrup
1 c. raisins
2 eggs, beaten

Cook and chop up liver. Cook rice in milk. Fry onion in lard, add liver, rice, salt and pepper. Stir in syrup, raisins and eggs. Bake in a moderate oven for about an hour. This makes a large pudding, and it's not too bad. Even if you don't like liver, you just may like this.

Liver and Bacon

4-8 slices bacon
1 lb. liver
2 T. flour
Salt & pepper
1 c. hot water

Put bacon in cold skillet and cook till crisp. Remove from pan. Roll liver in flour, salt and pepper. Fry quickly in hot bacon fat. Put on hot platter, put bacon on top. Pour off fat except for 2 T.. Stir in flour, add water gradually and boil 1 minute. Season and pour around meat. Liver should not be over-cooked, and should be served immediately. Try serving this with fried onions on top.

Italian Stew

1 lb. pork
Salt
1 qt. tomatoes
1 c. water
1 pkg. spaghetti, broken
1/4 c. grated cheese
A pinch of cayenne

Chop and salt pork and fry it till brown in a kettle. Add tomatoes, water and spaghetti. Cover tightly and simmer one hour, then add cheese and cayenne. This is very good.

Swiss Steak

1 c. flour
1 flank steak
1 onion, sliced
1 green pepper, sliced
1 qt. tomatoes
2 bay leaves

Pour flour on steak and pound with the edge of a heavy saucer until all the flour is used up. Brown onion in some lard in a roasting pan. Add steak and brown on both sides. Add green pepper, tomatoes, bay leaves and bake in a moderate oven about one hour. Remove bay leaves before serving.

The Rockefeller Center in New York was erected in the 30's across from St. Patrick's Cathedral.

Saw Mill Beef

1 4-5 lb. pot roast
1 lg. onion
1 c. tomato, chopped
Salt & pepper

Put roast into a heavy skillet (with cover). Smother meat with onion and tomatoes. Sprinkle with salt and pepper. Add a little water. Cover, roast for 4-5 hours. Check once in a while to see if it needs water.

Meat Balls

3 lbs. tender beef
1 onion, chopped
Salt & pepper
1/4 t. ginger
2 eggs, beaten
1 1/2 c. milk,
    scalded, cold
A little suet
1 c. bread crumbs

Put beef through the meat grinder 3 times. Add onion, pepper, salt, ginger, eggs, milk, suet and bread crumbs. Work with hands into a smooth creamy loaf. Form into balls and fry in butter. When done, add cream to make gravy. If you want these to be really round, put formed balls in the skillet and bake at 350 degrees for about 45 minutes.

Pot Roast

3-4 lbs. beef roast
Salt pork
1 onion, sliced
Flour
3 c. water
2 carrots
1/2 bay leaf
1/2 t. peppercorns

Wipe off the meat with a damp cloth. Fry salt pork and onion together until onion is soft. Sprinkle roast with flour and brown on all sides in fat. Put meat, on a rack, in a dutch oven; rinse out the frying pan and pour liquid over roast. Add remaining ingredients, cover tightly and bake slowly for about 3 hours. Make gravy from pan drippings.

Scrapple

Pork neck bones
1 1/2 qts. water
1 onion, sliced
Pepper
1 c. corn meal
1 c. cold water
1/2 t. salt

Simmer pork bones in water with onion and pepper for a few hours. Strain, reserving liquid. Pick meat from the bones and shred fine. Mix the corn meal with water and salt. Put pork stock in the top of the double boiler and stir in cornmeal mixture. Cook and stir over high heat for about 3 minutes. Cover and steam about 15 minutes, stirring once in a while. Add meat and mix. Put into a bread pan and let stand until cold and solid. Slice, dip in flour and fry in butter or lard.

This has been called "Crapple" by some unappreciative folks. Judge for yourself.

Slumgullion

4 slices bacon, diced
2 c. meat, cooked
1/2 onion, diced
1 can tomatoes
1 1/2 c. cheese, cubed

Brown bacon in a heavy saucepan, drain, and set aside. Fry onion in bacon fat over low heat. Stir and cook until onion is transparent. Add tomatoes, beef and bacon. Simmer 5 minutes. Stir in cheese. Pour into tureen and serve over fresh bread. If the family is getting anxious for supper to be ready, set the table. It will encourage them.

Goulash

1/2 lb. veal
1/2 lb. beef round
1/2 lb. pork
1 T. paprika
2 pr. pork kidneys
4 T. fat
2 onions, sliced
1 green pepper, shredded
1 c. tomatoes
1 sprig parsley
4 potatoes, peeled
Salt & pepper

Cut meats into cubes and mix with paprika. Soak kidneys in cold water for 1 hour. Drain. Plunge in boiling water 1 minute. Chop up and discard tough parts. Fry onion and green pepper in fat, add meat and kidneys. Brown all in fat. Add tomatoes and parsley. Barely cover with boiling water, cover pot and simmer for an hour. Add potatoes, salt and pepper and more water if needed. Simmer 30 minutes. If you wish, thicken liquid with 1 T. flour rubbed into 1 T. butter and cook until stew boils up.

Stuffed Peppers

3-4 green peppers
1/2 lb. veal,
  chopped fine
  (any meat will do)
1/2 c. bread crumbs
A little parsley
Juice of small onion

Cut tops off peppers and scoop out seeds. Soak in salt water while making stuffing. Brown meat. Mix well together with other ingredients. Season and moisten with gravy or soup stock. Stuff peppers and bake one hour in a moderate oven. From Mrs. Gilbert.

If the family is getting anxious for supper to be ready, set the table. It will encourage them.

1932: *Pretty Amelia Earhart crossed the Atlantic in her plane - solo - and stole the hearts of the American people.*

Cabbage Casserole

1 lb. ground meat
1 onion
Salt & pepper
1 can tomato soup
1/2 can water
1 small cabbage, cut up
1 c. rice

Brown meat and onion. Drain. Put into casserole and add salt, pepper, tomato soup, water, cabbage and rice. Stir till well mixed. Bake 2 hours at 350 degrees.

Veal Loaf

1 1/2 lbs. veal
A little salt pork, chopped
1 t. salt
1/2 t. pepper
1 t. sage
1 egg
1 c. bread crumbs
2 T. milk
A trifle onion

Mix all together well and form into a loaf. Set into a skillet, add a little water and bake in a slow oven (275 degrees) for about two hours. Cover the pan to keep loaf from drying out.

Hamburg Patties

1 lb. ground
    round steak
Salt & pepper
1-2 T. onion, grated
Butter
1 c. water

Mix meat and seasonings. Shape into thick cakes with slight depression in the center. Have frying pan hissing hot but with no fat in it. Sear meat quickly on both sides, reduce heat and cook until desired doneness, 8-10 minutes. Remove meat to platter, add water to skillet and stir well; pour over meat and dot with butter. Serve right away or the meat cakes will get tough.

Hunter's Stew

2 T. lard or suet
2 lbs. venison, cubed
Salt & pepper to taste
Water
6 carrots, chopped
3 stalks celery,
    sliced big
2 lg. potatoes, cut up
1 qt. tomatoes

Melt fat in large skillet. Season venison and add to fat, cover with water and simmer about 45 minutes. Add vegetables and simmer another 30-45 minutes until all are tender. Serve hot with biscuits to sop up the juices.

Meat Skillet

1 small onion, chopped
2 c. cooked beef, veal,
   lamb or chicken
1 thick slice bread
1 c. milk
1 1/2 t. curry powder
Salt to taste
1 T. lemon juice
Hot cooked vegetables

Put meat and onion together through food chopper, or mix thoroughly. Soak bread in milk and add both to meat; add eggs and seasonings. If curry isn't very salty, you might add some salt. Heat a little fat in the skillet, add meat and pat down flat. Cook slowly till brown and crusty on the bottom (you may have to add more fat.) Slice across center and fold in half. Put on serving platter and surround with vegetables; green beans, wax beans, carrots - whatever you like.

Swiss Steak

1 round steak
1/2 c. flour
Salt & pepper
2 T. fat
1 lg. onion, chopped
2 potatoes, halved
1-2 carrots, sliced
1 pt. tomatoes or
   3-4 fresh, chopped

Sprinkle meat with flour, salt and pepper and pound it with the edge of a heavy saucer until most of the flour is absorbed. Melt fat in skillet; sear meat well on both sides; remove from pan. Add onion and saute till tender. Return meat and add remaining ingredients. Simmer on top of stove, covered, for an hour or so until meat is tender. Add water if necessary. Or if you already have the oven on, bake at 350 degrees for 1 1/2 hours. This is good.

Stuffed Roast Racoon

1 lb. sweet potatoes,
  mashed
1/2 c. raisins
1 c. bread crumbs
2 apples, peeled
  and chopped
1/4 c. butter, melted
Salt & pepper to taste
A 4-5 lb. young racoon

First make the stuffing: mix together all ingredients (except racoon, of course) gently until blended. Set aside. Wash racoon meat thoroughly and dry with a cloth. Cut off some of the fat, leaving just enough for a thin layer. Salt the inside of the coon. Stuff gently with the sweet potato mixture and sew opening shut. Bake at 325 degrees for about 3-4 hours. When half done, turn over so all sides will be browned. Serve with a crisp vegetable salad.

1937: *Tom and Jerry cartoons appeared on the screen. Even though the films portrayed a lot of violence, the comedy, linked with the physically impossible circumstances, made the cartoons a hit.*

50

Roast Venison

4-5 lb. venison roast
6-8 slices bacon
1 sprig rosemary
1 c. water, stock or wine
1/4 t. ginger
1/2 t. cinnamon
2-3 cloves
1 1/2 t. sugar
2 T. bread crumbs
1 t. vinegar
2 T. butter

Wrap the bacon all around the roast. Put the rosemary in a heavy roasting pan and place the roast on top of it. Mix together the liquid, ginger, cinnamon, cloves and sugar; pour around roast. Season with salt and pepper. Roast in a moderate 350-375 degree oven for 2-3 hours. When done, remove from pan to serving platter; strain off gravy into a saucepan. Over low heat, cook juices with bread crumbs till boiling. Then add vinegar and butter; pour over roast. Serve with cranberry jelly.

How to Roast Lamb

Choose a roast that weighs at least 4 pounds. Wipe it off with a damp cloth and trim off fat; rub well with salt and pepper. Put in a heavy roasting pan, fat side up. If lean, put strips of bacon over the top. Sear in a hot (450 degree) oven until brown, then reduce heat and bake for about 35 minutes per pound of meat. A boned or rolled roast will take longer. When it's tender, put on hot serving platter and make gravy from the drippings: add water to pan and scrape up all juices and baked pieces, bring to a boil and thicken with flour and water mixed to a smooth paste; let boil a few minutes. Season to taste and strain.

Broiled Lamb

Slices of cold lamb,
    roasted or boiled
2 T. olive oil
1 T. lemon juice
Salt & pepper
Currant jelly

Cut slices of lamb about 1/2" thick from a part of the joint that's not too well cooked. Mix oil and lemon, pour over meat and let stand an hour (lemon makes the meat tender.) Place in broiling pan and cook about four minutes. Season highly, and serve with currant jelly.

Hot-Pot

2 lbs. stewing lamb
2 lbs. potatoes, cubed
4 onions, sliced
Salt & pepper
A little flour
Water or stock

Cut meat into pieces convenient for serving. Mix salt, pepper and flour; roll meat in mixture to coat. Put a layer of potatoes in a deep dish, then a layer of meat, next onion; repeat until dish is filled, ending with potatoes. Fill dish with water or stock, and bake 3 hours at 350 degrees, adding more water if needed.

Baked Lamb Chops

6 lg. potatoes
1 small onion, sliced
Salt & pepper to taste
6 lamb chops
Cold water

Peel and slice potatoes. Put them in a flat, open baking pan. Add onion, salt and pepper to taste. Cover with cold water. Place chops on top and salt a little. Bake at 350 degrees for about 1 1/4 hours.

Brown Stew of Lamb

2 lbs. lamb
2 onions, sliced
2 carrots
1 head celery
2 T. drippings
1 1/2 T. flour
1 1/2 pts. water or stock
Salt & pepper

Cut meat into small pieces. Melt drippings in fry pan and brown meat on all sides. Remove meat, put in flour and brown that also. Add stock or water and stir till boiling. Put in meat and prepared vegetables. Season to taste and cook very slowly for two hours.

Irish Stew

2 lbs. stewing mutton
1 1/2 pts. water
6 small onions, sliced
1 small carrot, sliced
8 med. potatoes
Salt & pepper

Have meat in bite size pieces, trimming off some of the fat. Put into a large kettle containing nearly boiling water. Add onions and carrot. Simmer very gently, as hard boiling will toughen the meat. After 1 hour, add potatoes. Season to taste and cook till potatoes are tender. Then serve all together on one dish.

Fried Rabbit

1 rabbit
Salt & pepper
Flour
1 T. butter
1 T. lard

Cut the rabbit into pieces and rinse quickly in cold water (do not soak.) Season the meat, roll in flour to cover. Have the fats very hot in the skillet, put in rabbit. Cover and let the rabbit get very done before browning the other side. A rabbit fried in this way will smell almost as nice as it tastes.

1938: *Pierce-Arrow introduced the first recreational vehicle - the "Model 8 Travel-Lodge."*

Rabbit Stew

1 rabbit
Cold water
1 t. salt
Hot biscuits
2 T. flour
1 c. milk or cream
Salt & pepper to taste

Cut up the rabbit and place in a kettle. Cover with water, add salt and boil until tender. Break open hot biscuits and put them on a platter; put on each one a piece of rabbit. Make a paste of the flour and a little milk, stir into pan drippings and let boil a minute. Add the milk, season and pour over the rabbit. Serve at once.

Hasenpfeffer

1 rabbit
Salt water
1 onion
12 cloves
Flour
Equal parts butter & lard
A little cinnamon
1 T. vinegar
More flour

Soak rabbit in salt water for several hours; rinse with clear water. Put in a kettle and cover with water, adding onion studded with cloves. When tender, remove from pot, roll in flour and fry in fats until brown. Just before it's done, add cinnamon and vinegar; cover and let smother a minute or two. Put rabbit on platter, make gravy with pan drippings and flour, then add cooking liquid from boiling the rabbit. Pour gravy over rabbit and serve.

Stewed Squirrels

2 squirrels
2 qts. boiling water
1/2 lb. fresh corn
1/4 lb. lima beans, fresh
3-4 tomatoes, chopped
1 1/2 t. sugar
2-3 potatoes, in chunks
1/2 onion, sliced
Salt & pepper to taste
3 T. butter

Cut the squirrels into pieces. Put into the boiling water along with the rest of the ingredients, except the butter. Cover and simmer for about 2 hours; add the butter and simmer another 15 minutes. Bring to a full boil, remove from stove and serve. By the way, grey squirrel is even better than red squirrel, and they are both better tasting when hunted in the fall. Young squirrels may be fried.

Jean Harlow was a sensational leading lady in the early 30's. One of her most memorable films was "Public Enemy", on the screen in 1931. She was in 29 films (including "shorts") in her brief career; she died in 1937 at the age of 26.

Venison Sausage

4 lbs. venison
1 lb. beef
2 lbs. lean pork
1 lg. onion
1/2 peck potatoes
   (about 4 qts.)
2 T. salt
1/2 t. pepper
1 t. allspice
Sausage casings

Grind together all the meats with the onion. Next grind the potatoes and mix them with the meats. Add spices and mix thoroughly. Using a sausage stuffer, fill casings - but not too full. Tie the ends with string; put into a large kettle of cold water and bring to a boil. Cook for about 1 hour, being sure to prick each sausage with a fork after boiling for 10 minutes. Drain and cool. Tastes best when fried in butter till casings are light brown.

Fried Rice

1-2 c. leftover rice
1/2 c. leftover ham
1 small onion, chopped
1 egg, well-beaten
2 T. soy sauce
2-4 T. butter

Melt a little butter in a fry pan. Add egg and swirl it around so it's very thin. Cook until set; remove from pan and cut into strips. Add more butter to the pan and saute onion a little. Add rice, ham and egg pieces and fry until hot. Season with soy sauce (sometimes called "chop suey" sauce.) This is delicious and can be made with bits of bacon or any leftover meat.

1931: *Shirley Temple began her career at the age of three. This "little darling" brought happiness to millions.*

Poultry and Fish

I wipe'd away the weeds and foam,
And fetched my sea-born treasures home.

HOW TO FRY WITHOUT SMOKE

1—Put Crisco into cold frying pan. To cook the food thoroughly (for example, a fish) without smoke or scorching, fry slowly, using enough Crisco to partly cover it. It will not require the constant attention frying does when only a little fat is used.
2—Put frying pan over low heat. As soon as Crisco is melted put in a small piece of bread.
3—As soon as bread starts to brown put in the fish. Cook slowly until fish is nearly done, then turn to brown the other side. With plenty of Crisco in the pan the fish is easily turned without breaking. If you wait until it is almost done,
4—Strain the Crisco into an empty can and use it for the next thing you want to fry. No one will know you have fried fish in it.

I fry all of these in a rather unusual way. I put into a cold frying pan enough Crisco to cover the bottom well when it melts. Then I put in the vegetables, add a little water, cover and let simmer until the vegetables are soft. Then I remove the cover and brown, adding more Crisco if needed and stirring occasionally. If you have never fried these vegetables this way, you will be surprised to find how delicious they are. Sometimes instead of browning them I add a little sweet cream and serve at once.

Cold boiled parsnips are delicious browned on both sides in Crisco. For parsnip fritters I boil and wash parsnips, and to each cupful add 1 beaten egg, 2 tablespoons milk and 1 tablespoon flour, salt and pepper to taste and drop by spoonfuls into hot Crisco and brown on both sides.

Mock oysters are delicious too. For each cup of grated raw parsnip we need 1 beaten egg, ½ cup sweet cream, 1 tablespoon each of flour and melted Crisco, and salt to taste. Mix and drop small spoonfuls in hot Crisco and fry slowly on both sides. This makes enough for 3 people.

Tomatoes, Cucumbers, Squash, Eggplant, Turnips, Corn

Raw tomatoes, cucumbers, squash, and eggplant are simply rolled in flour and fried on both sides until done. Cold boiled turnips, white or yellow, are very good when browned in Crisco on both sides.

In the summer, green corn cut from the ear, mixed with red and green sweet peppers cut fine, makes a delicious dish. Simmer in Crisco about 10 minutes in a covered frying pan, then remove cover and brown. This dish is especially delicious if a little cream is added.

You will find a great many interesting ways to fry potatoes explained in the cook book offered free on this page.

© 1926 P. & G. Co.

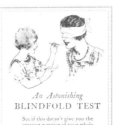

An Astonishing
BLINDFOLD TEST

See if this doesn't give you the greatest surprise of your whole cooking experience!

Put a little Crisco on the tip of one spoon. On the tip of another place a little of the fat you are now using; have someone blindfold you, and give you first one, then the other to taste.

Now did you ever imagine there could be such a striking difference in the taste of cooking fats? Think what an improvement Crisco's own sweetness and freshness will make in your own cakes, pies, biscuits, and fried foods.

Pineapples, Peaches, Bananas and Apples

Try fried pineapple or peaches with chicken. Cut peaches in half or pineapple slices in half, dust with flour and fry until soft and brown. Fry in plenty of Crisco, turning only once. Split bananas lengthwise, roll in flour, brown on both sides, dust with flour, add a dash of lemon juice and serve with ham, boiled or fried. Apples sliced, halved or quartered and browned in Crisco are delicious with pork or even as dessert when sugar is added.

Meat and Fish hints

Calves liver, pork tenderloins, cutlets of every kind, veal and lamb steak, chicken, and sweetbreads are all delicious when fried in Crisco.

All kinds of fish, whether whole, steaks, or shell fish, may be fried in Crisco to a lovely golden brown without a single unsightly break by the method you see pictured on this page.

Solving the problem of left-overs

Odds and ends of left-over meat, mixed with vegetables make most delicious casserole dishes. So do many of the cheaper cuts of meat—really far more nourishing and delicious than some of the more expensive cuts.

Take the raw or cooked meat, cut in small pieces, roll in flour, brown in the frying pan with plenty of Crisco and sliced onions. After browning add a little water and put in the casserole with left-over or fresh vegetables, such as potatoes, turnips, onions, green peppers or carrots. Add any left-over gravy or meat sauce and perhaps a bay leaf to improve the flavor. Cover and bake slowly two to three hours. Browning the meat in the frying pan gives a rich flavor, and the Crisco adds richness to the whole dish.

Winifred Paxton

Chicken Ala Stanley

1/4 c. butter
1 onion, sliced
1 chicken
1 1/2 c. water or stock
1 1/2 T. flour
1/2 c. cream
Salt & pepper

Melt butter and in it cook onion. Cut up the chicken into serving pieces and fry with onion for 10 minutes. Remove chicken; add flour and blend it with butter till smooth. Add stock or water, put in chicken and cook till tender. Add cream and seasoning just before serving.

Chicken Ala Providence

1 chicken
2 c. stock
2 T. butter
2 T. flour
1/2 c. carrots, cooked
1/2 c. peas, cooked
1 t. parsley
2 egg yolks
Seasoning

Cut chicken into pieces convenient for serving and boil gently till tender; season while cooking. Set aside while preparing sauce. Melt butter, add flour and blend smoothly; slowly add stock in which the chicken was cooked and stir until boiling. Cook 5 minutes, add carrots and peas, the egg yolks and season to taste. Pour over the chicken and sprinkle with chopped parsley.

Chicken Mousse

2 boneless chicken breasts
5 eggs
1 pt. whipping cream
1 handful flour
Salt & pepper

Grind chicken in meat grinder and pound until white. Add eggs, one at a time, and beat well. Add whipping cream gradually. Mix in flour, salt and pepper, and steam for two hours. Good with biscuits and creamed peas.

Chicken Pot Pie

1 chicken
1/4 lb. pork
1 qt. water or stock
Seasonings
Dumplings (next page)

Cut the chicken into rather small pieces and the pork into dice. Put in a good sized saucepan, cover with water or stock, cover and simmer 1-2 hours, according to the age of the chicken. Season when about 1/2 done. Put in the dumplings about 30 minutes before serving time. Cover closely till done. Pile the meat onto the center of a serving dish and put the dumplings around it. Be sure there is plenty of gravy.

Busby Berkeley awed audiences with his fantastic "kaleidoscope" dance routines involving scores of "girlies." His numbers were featured in 45 films during the 30's; one of the most well-known was "Forty-Second Street" in 1933.

Dumplings

1 1/2 c. flour
1/2 t. salt
1 1/2 t. baking powder
Milk
   (just enough to mix to
   a soft dough that will
   just drop from the spoon,
   about 2/3 c.)

Sift together flour, salt and baking powder twice. Add milk, mix quickly but thoroughly and drop by small tablespoonfuls into the hot gravy. Cook as directed in rule for Chicken Pot Pie. Some prefer to cook the dumplings separately and thicken the gravy with a flour and butter rubbed smoothly together. Suit yourself.

Fried Chicken

Lard/butter
1 large fryer
1 small onion, sliced
Flour
Salt & pepper
Allspice
Water

Put quite a bit of butter and/or lard in your frying pan or roaster. Brown the onion in the fat. Cut up the chicken, roll each piece in flour. Brown on both sides, season. Add a little water, cover and bake, turning once or twice to keep it from getting dry. This will be done in about 1 1/2 hours. The allspice really improves the flavor of both the chicken and the gravy.

Baked Chicken

1 large chicken
Lard
Flour
Salt & pepper
1/2 c. water
Butter, the size
   of an egg

Cut chicken into serving size pieces, wash and wipe dry. Put lard into spider, brown each piece slightly, roll in flour and place in baking pan; season. Put water and butter in spider, stir and pour this over chicken. Place in hot oven and bake 1 1/2 hours, basting occasionally. Veal chops and pork tenderloin are very nice baked in the same way.

Breaded Chicken

1 fryer, cut up
1 egg, beaten
Cracker crumbs
Salt & pepper
A few pieces butter
1 c. hot water

Crush cracker crumbs until fine. Dip each piece of chicken into egg, then in crumbs. Place in a baking pan, season to taste and add butter pieces. Pour the water into the pan and bake slowly.

1930: *Al Jolson starred in "Mammy," his famous "black face" film. In 1933 "Hallelujah, I'm a Bum" was released.*

Chicken Loaf

1 fowl
2 T. granulated gelatin
1/3 c. cold water
2 hard-cooked eggs
Seasonings to taste

Boil a fowl - an old one will do - till meat falls from the bones. Cool, strain, and boil liquor till reduced to 3 c. Remove meat from bones and skin, and lay meat in a mould, light and dark meat alternately, adding the egg slices. Soak gelatin in water for 1/2 hour, add the stock and pour over the meat. Set away to harden. Serve cold in slices. A good luncheon dish.

Creamed Chicken

2 T. fat
2 T. flour
1/4 t. salt
1 c. chicken stock
1 c. milk
2 c. chicken, cooked
2 eggs yolks
1/4 c. cream
1/2 t. lemon juice
2 t. parsley

Melt fat, stir in flour and seasonings and cook until bubbly. Slowly add chicken stock and milk; cook until thick and smooth, stirring often. Dice up chicken and add to sauce. Beat the egg yolks a bit and add the cream. Just before serving, add this to the chicken mixture and cook 2 minutes. Add lemon juice and parsley and serve immediately. This is even better when served over hot popovers. It makes it a bit fancier.

Southern Fried Chicken

2 broilers, halved or
  quartered
Salt pork or lard
  (not drippings)
About 1 c. flour
1 t. salt
1/2 t. paprika
1 T. flour
1/2 c. water
Cream

Wash and dry chicken. Slowly fry out fat, using enough to make at least 1/2" clear fat in skillet. (The secret is to use enough fat to keep the chicken moist and to brown it well.) Roll each piece of chicken in seasoned flour. Brown in hot fat carefully on all sides, and cook on the back of the stove, slowly, for another 20 minutes. Do not uncover. Remove to hot platter. Pour off most fat, add flour and scrape up all the pan drippings. Add water, cook and stir till smooth. Add enough cream to make a nice thickened pan gravy.

We had this a lot on Sundays; in the summer we also had potato salad and fresh lemonade while listening to the radio.

1932: *Walter Pitkin's "Life Begins at 40" was a best seller.*

How to Roast a Chicken

Remove any bits from inside dressed bird. Singe and remove pinfeathers. Wash under faucet. Dry inside and out. Stuff with a light hand with dressing of your choice. Turn wings across back, sew through wings and body with poultry needle and fine twine. Tie firmly, leaving long ends. Press thighs close to body and sew through; wrap twine around lower part of body and tie. Sew through ends of legs and tie close together. Sew once or twice through body opening if ragged. Rub with soft butter. Season well with salt and pepper. Mix about 1/2 c. butter and 1/2 c. water in a pan and keep hot for basting. Put bird on a rack in a roasting pan. Sear in a hot oven till browned, then reduce heat to moderate and bake until done, basting often. Make gravy from pan drippings.

How to Roast a Chicken Easier

Wash bird and cut into quarters, or leave whole. Put it in a roasting pan or skillet. Add 1/2 c. water. Bake at 325 degrees for 1 1/2 hours. Plain and simple and it turns out pretty good, too.

Roast Turkey and Dressing

1 large turkey
2 loaves bread
Salt & pepper
Sage
1/2 lb. butter, melted
4 large apples
1 small onion

Wash and dry turkey, inside and out. Peel and pare apples, chop into small pieces. Chop onion. Tear bread into small pieces. Mix all stuffing ingredients together gently. Stuff turkey with a light hand, stitch opening closed, and bake immediately for several hours at about 270-300 degrees.

Turkey Stuffing

Turkey liver
1/2 lb. veal
1/2 lb. suet
Salt & pepper
1 t. sage
1 small onion, chopped
1 gill soup stock (1/2 c.)
1/2 c. bread crumbs
20 walnuts
20 chestnuts

Cook liver and mince it fine. Make a force meat (grind together) of the veal and suet. Season to taste with salt and pepper, add sage, onion and cooked liver. Moisten with stock, add bread crumbs. Simmer on stove for about 15 minutes. Add walnuts and chestnuts to the mixture and stuff the turkey. This is a fine dressing.

1936: *Dale Carnegie's "How to Win Friends and Influence People" was the year's leading non-fiction best seller.*

Wild Rice Stuffing

1 loaf bread, dried & cubed
1 med. onion, chopped
1 t. sage
1 T. parsley
3-4 stalks celery, chopped
2 c. wild rice, cooked
1/2 lb. butter, melted in:
   1 c. water or stock
1/2 c. raisins

In a large mixing bowl, stir together the bread, onion, sage, parsley, celery and wild rice. Gently mix in the melted butter and water or stock. Toss in apple and raisins, if desired. Carefully stuff turkey or chicken; do not pack too tightly - keep it loose or the stuffing gets sticky. If you don't want to stuff the bird, bake the dressing separately in a covered casserole for about an hour. This is very good!

Some people claim that a stuffed chicken is a spoiled chicken, that the dressing absorbs much of the moisture and flavor from the flesh. Others prefer not to stuff a bird because it is easier and faster not to. For whatever reason, the dressing may be cooked separately and served with the bird.

Chestnut Dressing

Boiling water
1 1/2 lbs. French chestnuts
1/3 c. butter
Salt & pepper
1 c. dry bread crumbs
1/2 c. milk, scalded

Pour boiling water over chestnuts and let stand 5 minutes; remove skin with fingers and a knife. Cook nuts about 1/2 hour in boiling salted water. Drain, mash and add butter and seasonings. Pour milk over crumbs and add to nut mixture. Mix well, stuff bird.

Plain Dressing

1 c. dry bread crumbs
1 T. parsley
Grated rind of 1/2 lemon
1 t. mixed herbs
1/3 c. butter, melted
Salt & pepper
1/2 c. scalding
   water or milk

Crumble bread finely, add parsley, lemon rind, herbs, salt and pepper. Melt butter in water or milk and add, mixing well but gently. Fill the cavity of the bird with the dressing. For turkey, double all the ingredients.

Radio entertainment was never before readily available to people living in small towns and the countryside. Advertisers saw this as having far-reaching consequences.

1931: *The Star Spangled Banner officially became the national anthem.*

Potato Dressing

3 c. hot, mashed potatoes
1 c. dry bread crumbs
1 onion, grated
1 egg, lightly beaten
1/2 c. salt pork,
    finely chopped
1 t. sage
Salt & pepper

Have potatoes mashed quite finely. Add bread crumbs, onion, pork, sage, salt and pepper and mix with the egg. Use as a dressing for goose, duck or pork.

How to Roast a Duck

A domestic duck requires almost twice as much cooking as a wild duck. A wild duck will take about 30 minutes in a hot oven and should always have strips of bacon or salt pork laid across the breast while roasting, to keep it moist. Both kinds of duck need thorough basting; wild ducks are not stuffed.

Braised Duck

1 good-sized duck,
    an old one will do
1/4 lb. salt pork
1 carrot, diced
1 onion, sliced
1 bay leaf
A little parsley
3 c. hot water
Salt & cayenne to taste
2 T. each flour & butter,
    rubbed smoothly together

Truss duck as for roasting or cut into joints. Cut the pork into small pieces and fry. Add vegetables, bay leaf and parsley; cook 5 minutes. Put in duck and fry till browned. Place the whole works in a baking dish, add water, cover closely and cook in a moderate oven till tender, adding more water if need be. Dish up, and thicken gravy with flour and butter mixture. Season highly and serve with currant jelly or apple sauce.

Potted Pigeons

4 pigeons
1 1/2 pts. water or stock
1 stalk celery, chopped
1 slice salt pork
2 T. butter
2 T. flour
Salt & pepper

Clean and truss the birds as for roasting. Chop up the pork, fry out the fat and brown the birds. Put pigeons in a casserole, add celery, seasoning and stock. Cover closely and cook about 2 hours. Put birds on serving dish, thicken gravy with flour and butter rubbed together. Remove celery, and pour the gravy over birds.

Pheasant Pot Roast

1 pheasant
3 T. butter
3 T. flour
1/2 t. salt
1/4 t. pepper
2 c. water
1/4 c. black currant jelly

Roast Have bird clean and dry. Melt butter in large skillet and brown pheasant well on all sides. Remove from pan. Mix flour, salt and pepper and rub well into bird. Put in pan, breast up. Add 1/2 c. water and bring to boil. Let simmer, adding water as needed every 15 minutes. Cook about one hour till tender. Remove bird, place on platter. Stir jelly into pan; pass sauce at table.

When the weather was dry, there were more pheasants, because there wasn't any rain to flood out their nesting areas.

Prairie Chicken

1 young prairie chicken
Salt & pepper, to taste
2 T. lard
2 T. butter

Wash, cut up and dry bird; season. Have fat in frying pan very hot. Lay the chicken in and fry brown on both sides until tender. If the chicken is old, stew gently till tender and fry as above.

Pickled Fish

2 lbs. fish fillets
Salt
1 c. vinegar
1 c. water
Pickling spices
Onions
Sugar

Salt fish and leave overnight in ice box. Next morning wipe off. Boil the vinegar, water, spices and onions until the onions are done. Then put fish in vinegar mixture and boil for 3-5 minutes. Add 1 t. sugar for each quart. Good luck.

Frizzled Oysters

1 qt. oysters
3 T. butter
Salt & pepper

Dry oysters on a napkin. Heat butter in a frying pan and when very hot add oysters. Season and serve hot.

Baked Fish Mousse

2 c. raw white fish
1 c. soft bread crumbs
1/2 c. cream
2 T. flour
2 T. butter
1/2 t. salt
Pepper
4 egg whites

Skin and bone fish, chop fine. Mix crumbs and cream in a pan, heat and stir till bubbly. Rub flour and butter to make a paste, drop into hot cream and stir, cooking till thick. Add fish and season. When cool, fold in egg whites. Fill greased molds 2/3 full, place in pan of hot water and bake at 350 degrees till firm. Serve with a cream sauce with lemon.

Baked Stuffed Haddock

2-3 haddock fillets
1 c. bread crumbs
1/4 c. butter, melted
1 T. onion, chopped
2 T. hot water
Salt & pepper
8 slices bacon

Mix crumbs, butter, onion and water; season with salt and pepper to taste. Cut fish in halves, put a T. or so of stuffing on each piece, top with a slice of bacon. Put in a baking pan, add a little water and the other bacon. Bake in a 350 degree oven, basting occasionally.

Potato Fish Pie

1 1/2 lbs. fish
2 c. fish stock and milk
4 T. lard
1 clove garlic
3 T. flour
1 T. lemon juice
Salt & pepper
Parsley
Hot mashed potatoes

Cube fish, removing skin and bones. Put into a pan, cover with boiling water and simmer till fish is just tender. Drain, measure liquid and add milk to make 2 c. Fry garlic in lard for 5 minutes, remove garlic. Add flour, stir, add milk and stock mixture. Cook till thick and add fish and seasonings. Cover top with mashed potatoes and bake at 425 degrees until browned, about 15 minutes.

Escalloped Salmon

1 can salmon
3 c. cracker crumbs
2-3 T. butter
Salt & pepper
Milk

Butter a baking pan and put in 1/2 the salmon, a layer of cracker crumbs; sprinkle on salt and pepper and dot with butter. Add another layer of salmon and crumbs; pour over enough milk to just come to the top. Bake until hot.

Salmon Croquettes

1 can salmon
1 T. lemon juice
1 T. butter
2 T. flour
2 c. milk
Salt & pepper
2 egg yolks
1 T. cream
1 1/2 c. bread crumbs
More bread crumbs
1 egg, beaten

Free salmon from oil and bones. Shred it carefully. Melt butter in a saucepan and mix in flour; slowly add milk and seasonings. Beat egg yolks with cream and add to the milk. Add fish and bread crumbs and cook 3 minutes. When cold, shape into croquettes. Roll in crumbs, then in beaten egg, then in crumbs again. Fry in deep hot fat. Of course these are good - they're fried.

Salmon Chops

1 can salmon
2 t. butter
2 t. flour
1/2 t. salt
Dash cayenne
1 T. lemon juice
1 t. parsley, chopped
Macaroni
1 egg
Bread crumbs

Remove skin and bones from salmon, and mash fish with a silver fork. Mix together butter, flour, salt and cayenne; add the fish, lemon and parsley. Chill and form into "chops". Dip in beaten egg and bread crumbs, put a piece of macaroni in one end for a "bone" and fry in hot lard till brown on both sides. This is very good, but they'll know it's not pork chops.

Fish in a Dish

2 lbs. finnan haddie
3/4 c. evaporated milk
Black pepper
Butter
Parsley

Cut off tail, wash fish. Put fish in a large kettle, cover with boiling water and put on the back of the stove, so it will not boil, for 15 minutes. Drain and put fish in a baking dish. Sprinkle on pepper, dot with butter, surround with milk and bake about 20 minutes at 375 degrees. Spoon sauce over fish and sprinkle with parsley.

Fish Chowder

6-8 slices bacon
6 potatoes, sliced thick
1 can salmon
1 onion, sliced
2 c. milk
Crackers crumbs

Put bacon in the bottom of a kettle and fry a little. Add a layer of potatoes, a layer of salmon, more potatoes and the onion. Cover with water and simmer about 1/2 hour. Pour on milk and cover with cracker crumbs.

Baked Fish in Perfection

1 lg. fish
1/2 c. butter, melted
Juice of 1/2 lemon
Salt & pepper
1 T. onion, chopped fine

Split fish down the back, wipe it well and lay it in a greased pan. Mix butter and other ingredients together, and pour a little over the fish. Place in a hot oven and bake about 30 minutes, basting with prepared butter every 10 minutes. Serve very hot. Mmmmmm!

Perfect Fish Balls

2 c. potatoes, chopped fine
1 c. cod, flaked
1 T. butter
Pepper to taste
1 egg, beaten
Plenty of lard, smoking-hot
Fried bacon (optional)

Cook fish and potatoes till tender. Mash very thoroughly till every lump is gone. Add butter, pepper and egg, and beat till the whole is light and creamy. Take up, a little at a time, with a spoon dipped in hot fat (prevents sticking), and drop into hot lard. Cook till golden brown. If the lard is the right heat this will not take more than a minute. Drain well and serve with crispy fried bacon. (Or without it.)

Codfish Fritters

Strips of salt codfish
2 T. flour
1 egg, separated
1/3 c. milk
Hot lard

Cut fish into finger-sized strips and soak overnight in the ice box. In morning, drain and dry. Mix flour, egg yolk and milk, beating well to remove all lumps. Add frothy-beaten egg white. Dip fish in batter, one piece at a time, and fry at once in hot fat to cover. Cook till golden brown; drain well before serving.

Halibut Steak

2 halibut steaks
Salt pork, thin sliced
2 T. lemon juice
Salt & pepper
1/2 pt. oysters
2 T. butter, melted
1/2 c. bread crumbs

Wash and dry fish. Place salt pork in a pan, lay one fish steak on pork and pour on lemon juice. Season. Dip oysters in butter, then in crumbs, and put on top of fish. Place the second steak over the oysters and season as before, laying salt pork over all. Bake 30-40 minutes, basting often with pan juices and lastly butter. Remove pork from top, cover with crumbs, brown and serve.

Grampa liked this dish, and when Grandma asked him why he went fishing so much, he would always answer, "Oh, just for the halibut...."

Turbot

1 bass or white fish
1 pt. milk
2 eggs, beaten
2 T. butter
1 T. flour
Salt & pepper
Cracker crumbs

Boil the fish and pick it to pieces. Place in a baking dish and pour over it the milk, eggs, butter, flour and seasonings. Sprinkle cracker crumbs over the top and bake for about 20 minutes. This is good served with boiled potatoes and fresh vegetables; carrots or something colorful. Beets, maybe.

Baked Salmon

1 can salmon
1 c. milk
1 egg, well-beaten
Butter the size
of a walnut

Mince the salmon fine and mix together with milk, egg and butter. Bake in a quick oven and serve hot. May garnish with parsley and lemon slices, if you wish.

Gertie's Salmon Loaf

1 can salmon
1 c. cracker or
bread crumbs
1/2 c. butter
3 eggs, well-beaten
1 c. milk
Salt & pepper

Butter and flour a pan. Warm the milk and butter. Add salmon (picked fine), crumbs, eggs and salt and pepper to taste. Pour into the pan and put it in a double boiler and steam for 2 hours. Serve hot or cold. Excellent for sandwiches.

Baked Stuffed Fish

1 c. cracker & bread crumbs
1 t. salt
1/2 t. pepper
2 t. onion, chopped
1 t. parsley
1/4 c. butter, melted
1 good-sized fish
2-3 slices bacon
Salt & pepper
Flour

Mix crumbs, salt, pepper, onion and parsley together. Moisten with the melted butter and stir gently. Set aside. Clean and wipe the fish. Take out the backbone, and rub the fish with salt. Stuff, and sew together. Cut gashes 2" apart on both sides. Put narrow strips of bacon in the gashes. Rub all over with butter, salt and pepper. Dredge well with flour. Put into a hot oven without water. Baste when flour is browned and baste often. This is dandy good!

Hairstyles were more relaxed than before - gone were the severe Marcelles of the decade past. Again, women wanted to appear softer and more sophisticated.

1930: *Miniature golf courses popped up all over the country, creating another inexpensive form of entertainment.*

Lutefisk With Rice

1 c. rice
2 1/2 lbs. lutefisk
Water
1 c. cream
1 T. butter, melted

Cook rice. Boil lutefisk until done. Flake, remove bone, mix with rice, season to taste. Put in baking dish and cover with cream and butter. Bake until nice and brown. That's it.

Mrs. Gilbert's Salmon in Mold

1 can salmon
4 T. butter, melted
3 eggs
1/2 c. milk
1/2 c. crackers
Salt & pepper
Parsley

Drain liquor from the fish, set aside. Chop fish fine and mix in the butter. Beat eggs light and add crumbs. Mix well. Put into buttered mold and steam one hour. Season to taste with salt, pepper and parsley. Serve sauce below.

Sauce:
1 c. milk
1 T. cornstarch
Liquor from salmon
1 lg. T. butter, melted

Mix milk and cornstarch. Let come to a boil and cook until thickened. Add salmon liquor and butter. Put egg in last and carefully boil a minute to cook. Pour over salmon and serve. A fancy way to have canned salmon.

Fish and Mushrooms

1 lb. fish fillets
2 green onions, sliced
1 tomato, chopped
2 T. lemon juice
1/2 c. fresh mushrooms
1/2 t. salt

Put fish into a baking dish. Put onions, tomato, and lemon juice on fish. Slice up mushrooms and put them on top of other ingredients. Sprinkle with salt. Bake at 350 degrees for about 30 minutes until fish flakes and is done.

All-Day Fried Fish

Several nice pan-fish
1 c. flour
1 t. salt
Pepper
1/2 t. paprika
Butter

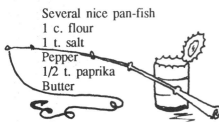

Go to your favorite fishing spot and spend the better part of the day fishing. Bring home the catch, clean (or better yet, have someone else do it!) Dredge fish in seasoned flour and fry in butter until flaky and tender. Serve with new potatoes and maybe some fresh peas. Watch for those bones.

Jigsaw puzzles were a popular diversion, and an inexpensive way to spend an evening. Even at parties, couples would sit for hours, hunched over the table, putting pieces together and talking.

Pickled Fish

Raw fish, chilled
2 T. salt
1 onion, sliced
1/2 c. sugar
2 t. mixed spices
White vinegar

You can use almost any type of fish, but northern and sunfish are good. Clean fish and cut into smallish pieces. Fill a quart jar 3/4 full of fish. Add salt, onion, sugar and spices - fill with vinegar. Cap tightly and refrigerate. Shake jar every day for 4 days; let set for a week or two for good taste. This keeps for a couple months.

Recipes to Remember

Vegetables

And God said "Behold, I have given
you every green herb bearing seed
which is upon the face of all the earth,
and every tree yielding seed; to you it shall be for meat."

71

Fancy Style Peas

2 T. butter
1 slice bacon
2 c. peas, fresh-shelled
8 tiny onions
1/4 c. cream
Salt & pepper

Cook butter and bacon about 5 minutes. Remove bacon, add peas and some water; boil about 15 minutes. Also boil onions in a little salted water. Crumble bacon. Drain peas and onions. Combine peas, onions, bacon, cream and seasonings. Heat through and serve.

Baked Onions

4 med. onions
1/4 c. butter, melted
Salt & pepper

Put onions on a tin and bake as for potatoes. When done, remove skins, pour on butter. Sprinkle with salt and pepper and serve hot.

Candied Sweet Potatoes

3-4 large sweet potatoes
1/3 c. butter
1 c. brown sugar
        OR
3/4 c. maple syrup

Peel and cut potatoes into thick slices. Boil until not quite done. Drain and put them in a baking dish. Heat butter and sugar or syrup; pour over potatoes and bake at 400 degrees for 30-40 minutes.

Italian Cauliflower

1 large cauliflower
2 T. butter
2 T. flour
1/2 t. salt
1 c. milk
Salt & pepper
1/2-3/4 c. grated cheese
Butter
Bread crumbs
Watercress or parsley

Wash cauliflower, put it in salted water and cook until tender. Meanwhile, make sauce: Heat butter and flour, stir till foamy. Slowly add milk; add seasonings and cook till thickened. Keep warm. Back to cauliflower: Carefully remove it with a skimmer, so as not to break it. Put on a platter, flower side up. Pour on sauce, sprinkle with cheese, dot on butter, top with bread crumbs and bake for 20 minutes at 350 degrees. Send to the table on the same dish. Garnish with watercress or parsley. This is an attractive way to serve a not-so-popular vegetable.

1935: Monopoly was on the market and people who played the game could experience, at least vicariously, instant wealth - or bankruptcy. Just like real life. It made you think you were pretty smart when you won.

Fresh Tomato Fry

1/2 c. flour
1/2 t. baking powder
1/2 t. salt
1 egg, beaten
1/3 c. milk
6 ripe, firm tomatoes
Salt & pepper

Sift together flour, baking powder and salt. Add milk and beaten egg; mix well. Slice tomatoes rather thickly, sprinkle with salt and pepper and drain. Dip tomato slices in batter, and fry in a hot greased skillet until brown on both sides. Good for breakfast or lunch, served with bacon.

Creamed Cauliflower and Green Beans

1 small cauliflower
1 c. green beans
2 T. butter
2 T. flour
1/2 t. salt
Pepper or paprika
1 c. milk (may
   be part cream)

Wash cauliflower and break into florets. Clean beans and cut into pieces. Cook together until tender. Meanwhile, melt butter, remove from stove. Add flour and seasonings; stir till smooth. Add milk slowly. Put back on stove, and stir and cook till sauce is smooth and thickened. Add cooked vegetables and heat through. Good with buttered bread crumbs on top, too.

Creamed Fried Onions

1 lb. Bermuda onions
Fat for frying
2 T. flour
1 1/4 c. milk, hot
Salt & pepper to taste

Fry peeled, sliced onions in hot fat until tender and fairly brown, turning frequently. Scrape up all the brown crispy parts, sprinkle on flour and stir gently till well mixed. Stir in hot milk and cook until boiled up. This is a surprisingly tasty dish. Serve with meat loaf or roast beef. Or steak!

Baked Parsnips

8-10 med. parsnips
2 c. milk
2 eggs
Salt & pepper
A little nutmeg
Butter

Boil parsnips in salt water until tender. Be careful not to overcook them as they get soggy. Cool; peel and slice longways and put in a baking dish. Mix milk, eggs and seasonings, pour over, dot with butter; bake at 325 degrees, 45 minutes.

"Charity begins at home," but it was no longer just a matter between family and neighbors. It became a part of the government - America taking care of Americans.

Fried Parsnips

6-8 small parsnips
2-3 T. butter
Salt

Peel parsnips and slice fairly thin. Heat butter in skillet; fry slices slowly until browned. Sprinkle with salt. These have a sticky-sweet characteristic that is oddly flavorful.

Raw Fries

6-8 potatoes
2-4 T. butter or lard
Salt & pepper
1 onion, chopped

Peel and slice potatoes. Heat fat in a large skillet till hot, add potatoes. Fry well, turning occasionally, until nice and brown. Add onion and fry a few minutes more. Season with salt and pepper. These are really good. The kids even like them.

Corn Pudding

2 cans corn
1 c. cracker crumbs
4 c. milk
4 eggs
2 T. sugar
A little nutmeg
Salt & pepper to taste
Butter

In a large bowl, mix together the corn, cracker crumbs and milk. Beat the eggs fairly well and add to the corn mixture. Add salt, pepper and nutmeg; stir well. Pour into a pudding pan or large baking dish and dot with bits of butter. Bake slowly in a warmish oven (about 300 degrees) for about one hour.

Lima Beans

1 lb. lima beans
Boiling salt water
2 T. butter
Pepper to taste

Shell beans into cold water and let lie 1/2 hour or longer. Drain and put into boiling water. Cook till tender. Drain; add butter and pepper.

Green Peas With New Potatoes

2 slices salt pork
1 lb. or so new
    potatoes
2 c. green peas
Water
Salt & pepper to taste
1-2 T. flour
1 c. milk

Dice up salt pork and fry a little in a kettle. Add potatoes, peas and enough water. When tender, pour off all water except about 1/2 c. Season with salt and pepper, add milk and thicken with flour. If you put the milk into a jar with the flour and shake it well, the sauce won't get lumpy.

Escalloped Potatoes

3 c. potatoes, cubed
1 t. salt
1/2 t. pepper
2 c. milk
2-3 T. flour
Grated bread crumbs
Butter

Put potatoes into a greased baking dish. Add salt, pepper, milk; sprinkle on flour. Cover with bread crumbs and dot with butter. Bake about 45 minutes at 350 degrees. You might want to garnish with parsley just before serving.

Potatoes With Cheese

6 med. potatoes
1 t. salt
2 T. flour
1/2 c. grated cheese
4 T. butter
Pepper
2 egg yolks, beaten
2 1/2 c. milk

Pare potatoes and cut in very thin slices. Cook 5 minutes; drain. Put about 1/4 of the potatoes in a baking dish, and sprinkle on about 1/4 of the salt, flour, cheese, butter and a little pepper. Continue for 3 more layers. Mix the yolks with the milk and pour over all. Bake for an hour until potatoes are tender and custard is set. Bake at 350 degrees.

Potato Souffle

2 c. hot, mashed potatoes
1/2 c. hot milk
Salt & pepper
A little nutmeg
2 eggs, separated

Beat egg whites until stiff. Beat yolks well and add to potatoes along with the seasonings. Fold in the whites, and put into a well greased baking dish. Bake at 400 degrees for about 25 minutes. (If you have leftover cold mashed potatoes to use up, add the hot milk to them and reheat in a double boiler and beat till smooth.)

Potato Chips

Use only mealy potatoes. Peel and slice potatoes as thin as you can. Soak in cold salt water (1 T. salt to 2 c. water) for an hour or more. Drain and wipe them dry with a towel. Be sure they're dry or the fat will sputter, and this could be dangerous. Have lard very hot - about 375 degrees - and dip frying basket in first, before adding potatoes, to prevent sticking. Fry a little less than a cupful at a time. Cook until light brown on both sides. Drain on absorbent paper and sprinkle with salt.

French Fried or Long Branch Potatoes

Peel good-sized potatoes and cut into strips about 1/4" or 1/2" wide. Soak in cold salt water for about an hour. Drain and dry thoroughly. Fry as for potato chips. When making a large amount of these for a crowd, fry them only until they are soft and tender, but not brown. Drain and keep warm until dinnertime. Then fry them again in lard at about 395 degrees. Drain, sprinkle with salt and serve right away, with ketchup if you like.

Spanish Rice

1 c. rice
1 qt. water
4 tomatoes
4 green peppers

Remove seeds from tomatoes and peppers; chop fine. Put in a double boiler with rice and water and cook for two hours.

Stewed Corn

4-6 cobs of corn
Salt & pepper
Sugar
Milk

Draw a sharp knife down the center of each row of corn; press out the pulp with the back of the knife. To each pint, add 1/2 t. each salt and sugar, dash of pepper and 1/2 c. milk. Heat and simmer 10 minutes.

Creole Tomatoes

4 lg. tomatoes
1 small onion, finely chopped
2 green peppers,
    finely chopped
Salt and cayenne
4 T. butter or drippings
2 T. flour
1 c. milk (part cream)

Cut tomatoes in half, crosswise; put cut side up on baking sheet. Sprinkle with onion, peppers, salt and cayenne. Put a bit of the butter on each piece, using 2 T. in all. Put 1/2 c. water in the pan and bake at 425 degrees till tender. Melt remaining butter and brown flour in it; add milk and the liquor from the baking pan; stir till boiling and cook 3 minutes more. Dish tomatoes on toast squares, pouring the sauce around them.

Baked Squash

1 squash
Brown sugar
Butter
Salt & pepper

Cut squash in half and scoop out seeds. Sprinkle cavity with about 1 T. brown sugar and 1 T. butter, season to taste and bake in a covered pan 1 hour at 350 degrees.

Corn Fritters

1 can corn
1 c. flour
1 t. baking powder
2 t. salt
1/4 t. paprika
2 egg yolks, beaten thick
2 egg whites, beaten stiff

Chop up corn. Sift flour, baking powder, salt and paprika; add to corn and mix. Add egg yolks and stir thoroughly. Fold in egg whites. Fry by spoonfuls in hot, fresh lard until light brown. Drain and serve hot.

Fried Egg Plant

1 egg plant
1 egg, beaten
1/2 t. salt
1/4 t. pepper
Cornstarch
Fat for deep frying

Pare and slice egg plant. Dip into egg mixed with salt and pepper, then into cornstarch, seeing to it that it's well covered. Fry to a deep, rich brown; drain on brown paper. Egg plant cooked in this way will be found very delicate and digestible.

Hashed Turnips

1 lg. yellow turnip
2 T. butter
1 t. salt
1/4 t. pepper
1 T. parsley
1/4 c. cream

Peel turnip and chop into small pieces. Boil until tender; drain and return to pan. Add butter, seasonings and cream. Let it boil up once and serve.

Ma's Baked Beans

2 lb. pea navy beans
1 c. white sugar
1/2 c. syrup or honey
1/2 t. mustard
1 pork "honk" (hock)
    OR
3/4 lb. salt pork,
    rinsed

In a large pot, cover beans with water and gently simmer about 20 minutes. "Just make them smile, don't make them laugh," Signe says. You'll know they're ready when you blow on them and the skins peel back slightly. Drain, save the water. Add remaining ingredients, just cover with saved water, and bake slowly, covered, 6-8 hours. Uncover pan last 3 hours. Add water as necessary.

1938: *The jitterbug appeared on the dance floor. Some people were delighted, others were pretty disgusted.*

Corn Oysters

1 c. green corn
3 T. flour, sifted
1/2 t. salt
1 egg
1/2 c. milk
Butter for frying

Scrape or grate corn from cob. Mix flour and salt with egg and milk to make a batter. Stir in the corn. Drop by spoonfuls into hot butter and fry until brown; Turn over and brown other side. Serve hot.

Baked Winter Squash

1 winter squash
Molasses
Butter, melted
Salt & pepper

Cut squash into 3" squares; remove seeds. Add 1/2 t. molasses and 1 t. melted butter to each piece; season to taste. Bake covered at 350 degrees for 1/2 hour - uncover and bake 1/2 hour longer. Serve in the shell with butter.

Baked Tomatoes

4 large tomatoes
2 T. butter
2 cloves garlic
1 T. onion, grated
Salt & pepper

Cut tomatoes in half crosswise and put into a greased baking tin. Melt butter in small skillet, add garlic and fry a few minutes. Remove garlic, add onion and cook till tender. Add bread crumbs and mix. Spoon on top of tomatoes, season to taste. Bake at about 375 degrees for 20 minutes or so till piping hot. Good for lunch.

Tomatoes With Mayonnaise

2 large tomatoes
Mayonnaise
Sugar

Peel tomatoes and cut in half. Put about 2 T. mayonnaise on top of each one, sprinkle with about 1 t. sugar. That's it and it's very good.

Zucchini Summer Squash

1-2 smallish squash
1 small onion, chopped
2-3 T. butter
1/2 t. salt
1/4 t. pepper
2 tomatoes, chopped
1 c. cheese, grated

Wash squash and slice in half lengthwise, then slice about 1/4" thick. Melt butter in large skillet; add zucchini and onion and fry until moisture is reduced. Add salt, pepper and tomato. Simmer about 10 minutes. Add cheese about 5 minutes before serving. Cover pan to melt cheese.

Carrot-Onion Glaze

1-2 bunches
   small carrots
1/2 lb. small onions
3 T. butter
3 T. sugar

Clean carrots with a scrub brush and cut longways into strips. Peel onions and prick with a fork so they won't break. Cook onions in boiling, salted water for about 15 minutes. Add carrots and cook until tender. Drain. Add vegetables to butter and sugar in frying pan and cook until shiny and brown. Good as a garnish for roasts, ham or chicken or as a side dish.

Spicy Sweet Potatoes

2 lg. sweet potatoes
1/4 c. nutmeats, chopped
2 T. butter
1/2 t. salt
1/8 t. nutmeg
1/8 t. cloves
Sifted flour
Fat for deep frying

Boil, peel and mash potatoes. Add nuts, butter, salt, nutmeg, cloves and cinnamon. Beat until well blended. Gently form into balls. Carefully roll in flour. Deep fry in hot fat until golden brown. Serve very hot. These are good with pork roast or chicken. Or they'll do just fine by themselves.

Stuffed Mushrooms

6 lg. mushrooms
1 c. soft bread crumbs
1 t. onion, chopped
Salt & pepper to taste
1/2 t. paprika
2 T. lemon juice
Butter, melted

Peel mushrooms and remove stems. Chop up stems and mix them with crumbs, onion, seasonings and lemon juice. Pour in enough butter to moisten mixture. Brush mushrooms with butter and place cap side down in a baking sheet. Fill rounding-full with mixture. Bake at 375 degrees until mushrooms are tender and black. These take a while, but they're worth it!

Salads & Salad Dressings

Almost anything that you can find,
Will make a salad to suit your mind,
Of fruit or fowl or flesh or fish,
You'll surely find here the one you wish.

French dressing is the most sophisticated of all salad dressings and it is also the easiest to make. The plain dressing may be varied by adding any seasonings or condiments that you like.

FRENCH DRESSING
3 parts Wesson Oil
1 part vinegar or lemon juice
Salt and pepper to taste
MIX WELL

Cheese Salad

1/2 c. mayonnaise
1/2 lb. cheese, grated
Celery salt
Pepper to taste
12 capers
Lettuce

Mix mayonnaise and cheese with seasonings. Form into balls with buttered paddles or 2 spoons. Serve on lettuce leaves on individual plates, garnish with capers. Pass more mayonnaise in a separate bowl.

Potato and Egg Salad

3 eggs, hard boiled
3 med. potatoes
Salt & pepper to taste
French dressing

Chop eggs finely with a silver knife to prevent discoloring. Cook potatoes with skins on; peel and dice. Mix with eggs, season and add dressing. Serve very cold on a bed of watercress.

Neufchatel Salad

1/2 lb. Neufchatel cheese
2 T. butter
1 t. parsley, chopped
1 t. chives, chopped
1 t. olives, chopped
Salt & paprika to taste

Beat cheese and butter till creamy. Add parsley, chives, olives and seasonings. Form into small balls and serve on lettuce or watercress with French or mayonnaise dressing. Serve very cold.

Tomatoes and Lima Beans

4 tomatoes
1 1/2 c. lima beans, cooked
1 T. parsley, chopped
2 T. onion, grated
1/2 c. nuts,
    chopped fine
2 T. celery, minced
Salt & pepper to taste
French dressing

Cut a slice from the top of each tomato and remove pulp with a spoon. Mix beans, parsley, onion, nuts and celery with French dressing to moisten. Fill tomatoes with the mixture and chill. Serve with more dressing. (Any kind of dressing may be used.) If you prefer, peel and slice tomatoes thickly and pile mixture on top.

1937: *The first full-length color cartoon was released. Give up? It was "Snow White and the Seven Dwarfs."*

Potato Salad

2 c. potatoes,
   cooked, diced
2 eggs, hard boiled, chopped
1 small onion, chopped
1/2 c. celery, sliced thin
1/2 c. cooked salad dressing
Salt & pepper
Paprika

Potatoes cooked "in their jackets" (skins on) are easier to peel and dice. Mix all ingredients in order given; chill completely. You might want to use equal parts of mayonnaise and cooked dressing for this.

Frosted Cheese and Fruit

3 oz. cream cheese
3 T. mayonnaise
2 T. lemon juice
1/2 c. evaporated milk,
   cold
1/2 c. dates, chopped
1/2 c. pineapple,
   crushed

Mash cream cheese, adding mayonnaise a little at a time. Add lemon juice to milk and whip hard till thick. Mix cheese and milk mixtures, fold in dates and drained pineapple. Pour into a mold, pack in ice and salt for 4 hours. Or freeze.

German Potato Salad

3 slices bacon, diced
1 egg
1/2 t. salt
1/2 t. sugar
1/8 t. dry mustard
2 T. vinegar
2 c. potatoes,
   cooked, diced
2 eggs, hard boiled
1 small onion, chopped

Put bacon in a cold skillet and fry slowly until it's very crisp and brown. Remove bacon from pan. Beat egg a little, slowly add vinegar and seasonings; mix well. Gradually pour into bacon fat, stirring constantly and cook till smooth and thick. Pour hot dressing over hot potatoes; mix quickly with the remaining ingredients and serve immediately. It's not too good cold, you know.

Devilled Egg Salad

6 eggs, hard boiled
1/2 t. dry mustard
     OR
2 T. prepared mustard
1/2 t. salt
Onion juice, if liked
Pepper & paprika
1 T. chili sauce
Cream or salad dressing to
moisten

Peel eggs and slice longways. Carefully remove yolks, so as not to tear the whites. Put yolks in a bowl and mash with a fork, making a paste. Mix remaining ingredients with yolks and blend till quite smooth. Lightly pile yolks back into egg whites. Chill; serve on lettuce with mayonnaise or your favorite dressing. Devilled eggs go very well with salmon.

Mixed Salad

1 clove garlic, halved
1 small head lettuce
3 tomatoes, cut
   in eighths
6 radishes, sliced
1/2 cucumber, sliced
1 small bunch green onions
1 T. parsley
1/2 c. French dressing

Have salad bowl very cold. Rub bowl with cut garlic. Break crisp, dry lettuce into bowl. Next, arrange tomatoes on top, then radishes. Add cucumber slices and onions, sliced thin. Sprinkle with parsley and chill at least a half hour before serving. At the table, pour on French dressing and toss gently using 2 forks, lifting from the bottom until well-coated.

Jellied Tomatoes

1 pt. canned tomatoes
2-3 whole cloves
1/2 t. worcestershire
1/2 t. salt
1/4 t. paprika
1 slice of onion
2 t. sugar
1 T. granulated gelatin
1/4 c. cold water

Cook tomatoes, with juice and pulp, seasonings, onion and sugar for 5 minutes. Mix gelatin with cold water, let stand till soft. Strain hot tomatoes, into gelatin, pressing out juice. Stir to dissolve gelatin. Taste, and add a few drops vinegar if it's too sweet, more salt if it's too bland. The seasoning depends upon how acid and flavorful the tomatoes are. Pour into a mould and chill until firm. Serve on lettuce with mayonnaise.

Salad Bouquets

1 large green pepper
Boiling water
Ice water
Romaine, center leaves
1 head bleached endive
1 small head
   Boston lettuce
1/2 bunch watercress
French dressing
1 T. chives, chopped

Slice off stem end of pepper; remove seeds. Pour boiling water over pepper; let stand 3 minutes; plunge into ice water. Cut into 1/4" rings with a sharp knife. Put an endive leaf on top of 2 romaine leaves; next put on a curly leaf of lettuce, then a spray of watercress. Hold firmly and slip a ring of pepper over stems, making a bouquet. Put each portion on a salad plate; pour over dressing; sprinkle with chives. Pretty fancy!

Contract bridge became popular during the 30's. Playing card sales were up and card games offered a variety of frugal entertainment. Other frequently played games were: auction bridge, 500, poker in all forms and Black Jack or 21.

Jellied Cranberries

1 T. granulated gelatin
1/4 c. cold water
1 c. boiling water
1/4 c. lemon juice
1/8 t. salt
2/3 c. celery, cut fine
1 c. sweet cranberry sauce

Let gelatin stand in cold water till soft. Add boiling water, stir till dissolved. Add lemon juice and salt; chill till thickened but not set. Fold in celery and sauce. Dip custard cups in cold water, pour in mixture. Chill to firm; unmold onto lettuce leaf; serve with mayonnaise. Good with chicken.

Cold Slaw

1 small cabbage
1 egg
1/4 c. vinegar
1/2 t. salt
1/2 t. mustard

Chop cabbage fine. Mix egg, vinegar, salt and mustard; cook until thickened. Cool thoroughly; pour over cabbage.

Chicken Salad

1 1/2 c. chicken cooked
2/3 c. celery, cut fine
3 T. French dressing
2/3 c. mayonnaise
Capers for garnish

Cut chicken into cubes; add celery. Stir in French dressing and chill for 1/2 hour. Blend in mayonnaise and serve on lettuce with a couple capers on top. This is also good with some green grape halves in it.

Cole Slaw

2 c. cabbage, chopped
2/3 c. cooked
    salad dressing
1 t. celery seed
Paprika

Chop or shred cabbage fine. Let stand in ice water 1 hour - this crisps it up. Drain. Mix in dressing and celery seed, sprinkle on paprika. Real cole slaw is never made with mayonnaise. Hmmm.

Harlequin Salad

1 c. red cabbage
1 c. reg. cabbage
1 c. peas
1/2 c. beets
1 onion, diced
1/2 c. carrot, diced
Salt & pepper
French dressing

Shave cabbage thin. Cook peas, beets and carrot till tender; drain and chill. Mix all vegetables, or arrange them in layers or heaps. The effect is better if they are mixed and they are also easier to season and to arrange. Pour on French dressing an hour before serving, keep cold. Pass more French dressing at the table.

Crabmeat Salad

1 c. crabmeat
1/2 c. celery
1 tomato, peeled
  & cut up
2 T. French dressing
Mayonnaise
Pimento strips
Green pepper strips

Pick over crab and take out any parchment-like tissue. Mix crabmeat, celery, tomato and French dressing; let stand in ice box 30 minutes. Blend in mayonnaise to moisten. Place on lettuce leaves, garnish with pimento and green pepper strips. If you want, use tuna fish or salmon instead of the crabmeat.

Poinsettia Salad

4 tomatoes
1 small onion, minced
1 stalk celery
1/4 green pepper
Mayonnaise

Scald, peel and chill tomatoes. Cut into sections almost down to the base, forming a flower. Mix onion, celery and green pepper, put in center of tomatoes and cover mixture with mayonnaise.

Stuffed Tomato Salad

6 ripe tomatoes
1/2 pt. cream dressing
2 cucumbers, diced
Lettuce
Salt & pepper
Parsley

Scald tomatoes; remove skins. Cut a slice from the top of each and remove seeds with a teaspoon. Season cucumbers well and mix with at least 1/2 the dressing. Fill tomato cups with mixture, put a spoonful of dressing on top and sprinkle with parsley. Serve on a bed of lettuce leaves.

Candlestick Salad

4 pineapple slices
Lettuce leaves
2 bananas
1/4-1/2 c. whipped cream
2 cherries
Mayonnaise

Place pineapple slices on lettuce leaves. In the hollow center, place 1/2 banana so that it stands upright. Put a spoonful of whipped cream on top and on that a cherry - ripe or preserved. Serve with sweetened mayonnaise.

Sunflower Salad

2-3 oranges
Lettuce leaves
1/2 banana
Whipped cream
Nut meats, chopped
Mayonnaise

Divide oranges into sections, removing as much skin and tissue as possible. Place on lettuce leaf in the shape of a sunflower. Use a thick slice of banana for center, spoon on whipped cream and nuts. Serve with sweetened mayonnaise.

Salmon Cuke Salad

1 head lettuce
2 cucumbers, sliced
1 onion, minced
Salt & pepper
1 c. salmon, shredded
Boiled dressing

Break apart lettuce, wash and dry leaves and place on salad plates. Put on cucumber slices, minced onion, salt and pepper. Beat together salmon and boiled dressing; pour over vegetables.

Fruit Salad

2 T. sugar
1 c. pineapple
3 oranges, peeled
1 pt. raspberries
3 bananas, sliced
2 c. whipped cream

Sprinkle sugar on pineapple and orange slices; let stand 1 hour. Alternate the fruit in layers and pour over all whipped cream when ready to serve. Serve very cold.

Fruit Salad

6 apples
3 bananas
1 c. walnuts
1 c. sugar
1 c. whipped cream
1 t. vanilla

Cut apples into small pieces; slice bananas, chop walnuts fine. Sprinkle with sugar; stir gently. Mix whipped cream with vanilla and stir into fruit. A few white grapes make a nice addition. Serve chilled.

Perfection Salad

1 envelope gelatin
1/2 c. cold water
1 pt. boiling water
1/2 c. mild vinegar
Juice of 1 lemon
1/2 c. sugar
Pinch of salt
2 c. celery chopped fine
1 c. cabbage, chopped
2 pimentos, minced

Soak gelatin in cold water for 5 minutes. Add boiling water, vinegar, lemon, sugar and salt; stir till dissolved. Mix in vegetables and pour into molds; chill until firm. Unmold and serve on lettuce leaves with your favorite dressing or pass a bowl of mayonnaise. This salad makes a pretty addition to your meal.

1933: Franklin Delano Roosevelt was elected president. Roosevelt was such a success that he would become the most re-elected president in history.

Cherry Salad

2 c. cherries, pitted
1/2 c. almonds, blanched
French fruit dressing
Lettuce leaves

Pit your favorite variety of ripe cherries. Shred almonds, mix with cherries, moisten with French fruit dressing and serve on lettuce leaves. Delicious with cold meat, broiled chops or chicken for a luncheon.

Mayonnaise Dressing

1 egg yolk
1/2 pt. olive oil
4 T. lemon juice
OR
4 T. vinegar
1/2 t. salt
1/4 t. paprika
OR
1/4 t. white pepper

Beat yolk in a cold dry bowl. Add the oil a few drops at a time until egg begins to thicken. Then add oil a little more rapidly until a teaspoonful at a time may be stirred in. Stir continuously with a wire beater while the oil is being added. Add the vinegar slowly, continuing to beat it constantly as it is being mixed. Add the seasonings at the very last. Keep in a cool, dark place.

French Dressing

1/4 t. salt
1/4 t. paprika
OR
1/4 t. pepper
1 t. prepared mustard
4 T. olive oil
1 1/2 T. vinegar

In a shallow dish, mix salt and pepper. Add mustard and oil; stir well to mix. Add the vinegar a little at a time, beating the mixture continuously with a fork. Serve as soon as it is mixed well.

Horseradish Dressing

1 c. heavy cream
1 T. grated or
    evaporated horseradish
2 T. lemon juice
Salt & paprika

Beat cream till quite thick; add horseradish. (If evaporated horseradish is used, mix it with a T. cold water and allow it to be absorbed before adding to cream.) Pour in lemon juice slowly, stirring constantly. Season, serve very cold. This is especially good with tomatoes.

The expansive nature of radio broadcasting made it an attractive medium to many merchants, especially when their products were associated with or endorsed by famous actors and actresses from Broadway and Hollywood, by big bands and by radio newscasters.

Boiled Salad Dressing

2 T. butter
2 eggs
2 t. sugar
1 t. dry mustard
1/2 t. salt
1/4 t. pepper
1 c. vinegar

In the top of the double boiler put the butter, eggs, sugar, mustard, salt and pepper. Cook over hot water until they being to thicken. Stir in the vinegar and continue cooking 3 minutes. Remove from heat; beat occasionally while cooling. Keep in a cool, dark place. This dressing will remain good for several weeks.

Cream Dressing

1/2 t. salt
1 T. flour
1 t. dry mustard
1 T. sugar
2 T. butter
2 egg yolks
3/4 c. cream
1/4 c. vinegar

Mix salt, flour, mustard and sugar in the top of the double boiler. Add butter and stir till mixed. While beating, add the egg yolks; stir well. Add the cream, and lastly add the vinegar. Cook over hot water until it thickens. Strain if necessary. Chill and serve cold.

Cooked Salad Dressing

1/2 c. sugar
3 T. flour
1/2 t. mustard
1 t. salt
1/2 t. paprika
1/8 t. white pepper
2 eggs, well beaten
1/2 c. vinegar
1/2 c. water
1/4 c. butter, melted

Mix dry ingredients thoroughly. Beat eggs in the top of the double boiler and add dry ingredients. Add vinegar and water slowly, stirring to keep the mixture smooth. Stir and cook until dressing is thick and smooth, about 10 minutes. Add the butter and mix well. Cool and store in the refrigerator. Use on potato, vegetable or mixed fruit salads.

Mayonnaise

1 c. salad oil
1 egg
OR
2 egg yolks
2 T. lemon juice
OR
2 T. vinegar
Salt & pepper
Paprika

Beat egg or egg yolks with a rotary beater until slightly thick; add 1 t. oil at a time, beating well between each addition, until 1/3 c. has been added. Add a few drops lemon or vinegar. The mixture should be quite thick and perfectly smooth. If it isn't, you added the oil too fast or didn't beat it well enough. Continue to add oil and acid alternately until it's used up. Add seasonings to taste. Store covered in the refrigerator.

French Dressing

1/2 c. salad oil
A little scraped onion
1/4 t. mustard
1/2 t. paprika
1/2 t. salt
A little pepper
1 t. sugar or honey
2 drops Worcestershire
2 T. lemon juice

Mix all ingredients together and beat well. Or you can put ingredients into a covered jar and shake hard until blended. Keep in a cold place. A milder dressing may be made by omitting the onion, mustard and Worcestershire sauce. The seasonings are a matter of personal preference. Instead of lemon juice, you may wish to use cider vinegar; or for a pleasant change, tarragon vinegar. Always serve French dressing cold.

Salad Crusts

Cut whole wheat bread into very thin slices. Spread with butter, mustard and a thin layer of grated cheese. Cover with another slice of bread, cut into finger lengths. Brown in the oven and serve with your salad.

Salad Dressing

2 T. flour
2 T. sugar
1 t. dry mustard
1/2 t. salt
2/3 c. vinegar
1/3 c. water
2 eggs, well-beaten
1 t. butter

In a saucepan mix flour, sugar, dry mustard and salt. Stir in the vinegar and water; add the eggs. Cook, stirring all the while, until thick. Add butter; chill. You may want to thin this with a little cream when ready to use, as it does get pretty thick.

A Simple Dressing

1/2 c. vinegar
1/4 c. oil
Juice of 1/2 lemon
1 small onion, minced
1/3 c. ketchup
2/3 c. sugar
1/2 t. paprika
1 scant t. salt

Beat all ingredients together with a rotary beater or wire beater. Or you can put it in a jar, cover and shake well. This is a fine dressing to use on lettuce and fresh tomatoes.

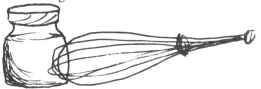

1938: *Perry Como performed on his first radio broadcast. His soft, soothing singing soon won him the title of "Mr. Calm."*

Mrs. L.'s Mayonnaise

3 egg yolks
Pinch of salt
Dash of paprika
1 pt. oil, or more
Juice of 1 lemon

Slowly stir eggs, salt and paprika in a cold bowl with a silver fork until yolks are mixed. Add oil drop by drop, stirring always, and in the same direction. When it looks oily, add a drop of lemon juice. Continue this oil/lemon process until used up. Three egg yolks will take at least a pint of oil and maybe more. If you do not want as much dressing as this, just use fewer eggs.

Chapman's Mayonnaise

2 egg yolks
1 c. oil
Juice of 1/2 lemon
2 t. tarragon vinegar
Seasonings

Method: beat eggs first, add oil drop by drop till half used, then faster. Then add acid slowly, beating all the time. May add whipped cream or not as desired; add seasonings. Will not curdle if this method is used. Store in refrigerator.

Boiled Dressing

4 eggs (may use 4 yolks
    or 2 whole eggs)
1/4 c. vinegar
4 T. butter, melted
A little onion juice
1/2 t. salt
2 t. sugar
1/2 t. dry mustard
1/2 t. paprika
Dash pepper
Few drops Worcestershire
Whipped cream

Slightly beat the eggs, add vinegar and lemon juice and cook in the top of the double boiler very slowly until quite thick and smooth. (If you don't have a double boiler, you can use a bowl set into a teakettle of water.) Remove from heat; stir in butter while hot. Season with onion juice, salt, sugar, mustard, paprika, pepper and Worcestershire sauce. Stir well until blended. Chill well, then add whipped cream to make it the desired thickness. This will keep any length of time if put in a glass, covered jar and kept cool.

1930: *Our friend, the Hostess Twinkie, was invented in Chicago by Jimmy Dewar.*

Breads and Biscuits

O, weary mothers mixing dough,
Don't you wish that food would grow?
Your lips would smile I know to see
A cookie bush or a pancake tree.

Why "Kitchen-tested" flour always gives you perfect baking results!

*..... a flour that always acts the
same way in your oven ..... a
flour that actually cuts
baking failures right
in half*

A Welcome Treat at Any Meal

Gold Medal Date Muffins—one of the
many delicious recipes constantly being created in the Gold Medal Kitchen. "Kitchen-
tested" recipes with "Kitchen-tested" flour—
perfect results every time you bake! Send for
these unusual recipes. Read our special offer.

TOO many women take
the blame upon themselves
when their baking turns out badly. More
often than not—you can blame the flour!

Because—ordinarily—a brand of flour may
often act "contrary" in your oven. Thus it
may spoil all your painstaking efforts.

But at last—the Gold Medal Millers have
found the way to end all such costly tragedies.

It is called the Gold Medal "Kitchen-test."
It is the one *sure* proof a flour will always
act the same way in your oven.

How flour acts

More than half of all baking failures can be traced to the way
flour behaves in your oven. To its
"contrariness."

So a miller has but one sure way of
knowing how his flour will act for you.
By "Kitchen-testing" it! By baking
with samples from each batch first.

This is the "Kitchen-test" all Gold
Medal Flour must pass—before any
of it can leave the mills.

How "Kitchen-test" is made

Each day the Gold Medal Kitchen bakes
with samples from each batch of Gold Medal
Flour milled the day before.

Each sample must bake the same perfect way
as all the others. Each batch must prove its uni-
formity before it is allowed to enter your home.

Now—one uniform flour for *all* baking,
from simple biscuits to fine cakes and pastries.
The same perfect results—always!

Guarantee

If at any time Gold Medal Flour does not give
you the most uniform good results
of any flour you have ever tried—
you may return the unused portion
of your sack of flour to your grocer.

He will pay you back your full purchase price. We will repay him. So
make this trial. Order a sack from
your grocer today.

Special Offer— "Kitchen-tested" Recipes

Why Not Now? As we test the flour in our kitchen,

we also create and test delightful new recipes.
We have printed all "Kitchen-tested" recipes
on cards and tiled them in neat wooden boxes.

These Gold Medal Home Service boxes
cost us exactly 70c each. We will send you
one for that price. And as fast as we create
new recipes we mail them to you free.

If you prefer to see first what the recipes are
like, just send us 10c to cover cost of packing
and mailing.

Check coupon for whichever you desire.

GOLD MEDAL FLOUR – *Kitchen-tested*

MILLED BY WASHBURN CROSBY COMPANY, MINNEAPOLIS, MINN., ALSO CREATORS OF WASHBURN'S PANCAKE FLOUR, GOLD MEDAL CAKE FLOUR, WHEATIES AND PURIFIED BRAN

Tune in on Gold Medal Radio Station
(WCCO—416 5 meters) at St. Paul-Minne-
apolis. Interesting programs daily. Also

communities for service...eMice, Wed
and Fri. at 10:45 am, the new Cookie,
Gold Medal Flour Home Service Dept.

"Service is the Northwest"

Dumplings

2 c. flour
1 t. salt
1 1/2 c. chicken
    broth, boiling
1/2 c. flour
1-2 qts. chicken broth

Mix together well to make a soft dough. Put the 1/2 c. flour on a bread broad; put dough on top. Let cool enough to handle. Then roll like pie crust. Cut in 1" x 2" strips. Let these dry 15 minutes. Drop into boiling chicken broth and simmer for 15-20 minutes.

Biscuits

2 c. flour
4 t. baking powder
3 T. butter
1/2 t. salt
3/4 c. milk

Mix dry ingredients and butter with 2 knives as for pastry. Add milk and mix. Roll out an inch thick. Cut in rounds, brush over tops with melted butter. Bake about 15 minutes in a 350 degree oven.

Corn Pone

1/2 c. shortening
1 1/4 c. sugar
2 eggs
2 t. baking powder
1 c. corn meal
Milk

Cream shortening and sugar, beat in eggs. Stir in baking powder, corn meal and enough milk to make a light cake batter. Bake in a slow oven (300 degrees) until it tests done, 45 minutes to an hour.

Mom's Whole Wheat Bread

3 c. warm water
1/4-1/2 c. molasses
2 T. dry yeast (1 cake)
1/4 c. lard, melted
7-8 c. whole wheat flour

Combine water, molasses and yeast in large bowl; let stand 5 minutes. Add lard and 5 c. flour. Beat about 110 strokes. Add more flour to make a stiff dough. Knead till smooth and elastic. Let raise till double. Punch down, cover, let raise again. Form into 3 loaves; place in well- greased pans; bake at 350 degrees for about 50 minutes.

1935: *James Stewart was on his way to become one of America's much-loved heroes in his first film, "Murder Man." Perhaps his most significant film of the era was "Mr. Smith Goes to Washington," released in 1939.*

Mollie's Nut Bread

2 c. white flour
1 t. salt
4 t. baking powder
1 c. sugar
1 egg
2 c. whole wheat flour
2 c. milk
1 c. nuts

Sift white flour, salt, baking powder and sugar. Mix with the graham flour. Add milk slowly, then the beaten egg. Beat well. Add nuts. Pour into greased tin and let stand for 20 minutes. Bake in a 350 degree oven.

Spoon Bread

2 c. corn meal
2 1/2 c. water, boiling
1 1/2 t. salt
1 T. sugar
2 t. baking powder
2 egg yolks, beaten
3/4-1 c. milk
3 T. butter, melted
2 egg whites, beaten

Pour water over corn meal, stirring all the while. Let cool. Mix salt, sugar and baking powder into egg yolks; add milk. Stir this into corn meal, beating vigorously. Add butter and fold in the egg whites. Pour into a well-greased deep baking dish. Bake at 400 degrees for about 40 minutes. Spoon onto plates from baking dish and eat while warm with butter.

Mother's Everyday Bread

2 cakes yeast
1 t. sugar
5 c. warm water
4 t. salt
3/4 c. sugar
1/2 c. + 2 T. fat
About 16 c. flour

Dissolve yeast and sugar in 1/2 c. water; set aside for 10 minutes. Mix together with the yeast the rest of the water, the salt, sugar and about 6 c. flour. Beat well, then keep adding flour until a stiff dough is formed. Knead well about 10 minutes. Cover, let rise. Punch down, cover, let rise again. Put into greased pans, let rise 1/2 hour, bake at 350 degrees for about 50 minutes. Makes 5-6 loaves - enough for a week if you're lucky! Mmmmm!

Plain Nut Bread

1 egg
2 c. sweet milk
Pinch of salt
1 c. sugar
4 c. flour
4 T. baking powder
1 c. walnuts, chopped

Beat egg until very light. Add milk, salt and sugar, beat until well mixed. Sift together flour and baking powder; stir into liquid mixture. When blended, stir in chopped walnuts. Pour into a greased pan and bake in a 350 degree oven for nearly an hour.

Raisin Nut Bread

2 T. butter
1/2 c. sugar
1 egg
1 t. baking soda in
   1 1/2 c. sour milk
Pinch of salt
1 1/2 c. graham flour
1/2 c. white flour
1/2 c. raisins
1/2 c. nuts, chopped

Cream together the butter and sugar; add the egg. Mix in soda-in-milk. Sift together salt and flours; add to batter. Stir in raisins and nuts. This makes a rather thin batter. Pour into greased tin and bake for about an hour at 350 degrees.

Corn Dodgers

2 c. corn meal
Boiling water
1 T. shortening
1 egg, beaten
2 T. milk
1 t. salt

Place corn meal into a bowl; pour in enough boiling water to moisten, stirring all the while. Add shortening, stir, and let cool. When cold, add egg, milk and salt. Bake in greased muffin tins at 350 degrees for about 20 minutes, or fry on the griddle.

Peanut Butter Muffins

2 c. flour
1 T. baking powder
1/3 c. sugar
1 t. salt
2 eggs
1/4 c. peanut butter
2/3 c. milk
1/2 c. water
2 T. butter, melted

Sift together flour, baking powder, salt and sugar. Beat eggs; add peanut butter, milk, water and butter; beat well. Add peanut butter mixture to flour mixture, beating only until blended. Grease muffin tins and fill 2/3 full. Bake in a 400 degree oven for about 20 minutes. Serve with butter and grape jelly - the kids really like this!

Raised Sally Lunn

1 cake yeast
2 T. sugar
1 c. milk, scalded
1/4 c. butter, melted
2 eggs
1/2 t. salt
3 c. flour

Put yeast and sugar into a large bowl; pour on lukewarm milk; let set 10 minutes. Beat in butter and eggs. Sift together flour and salt, add to batter. Pour into well greased pans, cover and let rise till double, about 45 minutes. Sprinkle with sugar and bake at 400 degrees for about 25 minutes. Break into pieces while warm and serve with butter.

Nut Bread

2 c. sour milk
1 t. baking soda in
    hot water
1/2 c. white sugar
1/2 c. brown sugar
1/4 t. salt
1 c. white flour
2 1/2 c. graham flour
1 c. raisins
1 c. nuts, chopped

Beat together the sour milk and soda; add sugars and mix. Sift together the salt and flours; add to batter. Stir in raisins and nuts. Stir good and let stand 30 minutes. Stir again; pour into greased pan and bake at 350 degrees for about 40 minutes.

Basic Biscuits

2 c. flour
1/2 t. salt
4 t. baking powder
2 T. shortening
About 3/4 c. milk
    OR
Milk & water, mixed

Sift dry ingredients; rub in the shortening as lightly as possible with fingers until just blended. Have milk as cold as possible. and mix with flour to form a soft dough. Mix with a flexible knife rather than a spoon, as the steel blade is colder than a spoon and also because the knife cuts and mixes more thoroughly. Turn out onto a well-floured board; pat to 3/4" thick. Cut into rounds; put on a baking pan, being sure they do not touch. Bake at 425 degrees 12-14 minutes.

The chief requirements for "good biscuits" are: 1. A very soft dough, so soft as to be almost sticky; 2. Very little handling, because much manipulation destroys their lightness; 3. A very quick oven. If "biscuits" are not allowed to touch each other in the pan, they will be lighter and more delicate than when placed close together.

Sweet Rolls

1 recipe of
    Basic Biscuits
Butter
Brown Sugar

Make biscuits into a loaf; let raise. Roll out 1/4" thick; spread with a thick layer of butter, cover with sugar. Roll up and slice 1" thick. Let raise, bake at 350 degrees 20-25 minutes.

Despite the dark despair of the Depression, Americans nevertheless enjoyed an at least "normal" number of new artists; stars of stage and screen, radio celebrities, heroes, comedians and villains. The American spirit carried on.

Cheese Biscuits

1 recipe of
  Basic Biscuits
2-4 T. cheese, grated

Make Basic Biscuits, adding cheese to dough. Bake the same way.

Parker House Rolls

1 recipe of
  Basic Biscuits
2/3 c. milk
2 t. sugar
Melted butter

Make biscuits, except use 2/3 c. milk; add sugar. Roll out 1/3" thick, cut into rounds, brush with butter, crease across centers; fold in half. Bake as directed.

Coffee Bread

1/4 c. butter
1 c. sugar
1 egg
1 1/2 c. milk
1 T. baking powder
2 3/4 c. flour
1 T. vanilla
4-5 apples, cored
1/2 c. sugar
1 T. cinnamon
1 T. flour
2 T. butter

Cream together the butter and sugar; add the egg and beat well. Beat in the milk and baking powder. Sift flour and add to batter; add vanilla. Grease a large baking pan and press in dough. Slice up apples and place in rows on top of dough. Then mix the sugar, cinnamon, flour and butter until well blended. Spread on top over apples. Bake in a 350 degree oven for an hour or so. Serve warm with cream poured over pieces.

Maple Rolls

1 1/2 c. flour
1 T. baking powder
1/2 t. salt
2 T. butter
About 3/4 c. milk
Scraped maple sugar

Sift dry ingredients; rub in butter. Add enough milk to make a soft dough. Roll out about 1/3" thick; spread thickly with maple sugar. Roll up, jelly roll style, and slice with a very sharp knife. Lay slices on a greased baking pan; bake at 350 degrees for about 15 minutes.

Loretta Young, with her beautiful complexion, was a natural to do ads for Lux Soap: "It does leave your skin like velvet!"

Fancy Coffee Bread

2 c. milk, scalded
1 yeast cake
2 egg yolks, beaten
1 t. salt
1/2 c. sugar
A pinch of cardamom
About 5-6 c. flour
1/2 c. butter

Cool milk until luke warm. Add yeast and 1 t. of the sugar; let stand 10 minutes. Add egg yolks, salt, sugar and cardamom; mix well. Stir in flour to make a soft dough. Let raise about 1 hour. Roll out dough quite thin, adding more flour if necessary. Spread dough with butter; cut into 3 strips; fold each strip so that butter is inside; braid the strips. Cut into loaves or make a wreath. Let raise again about 1 hour; brush top with egg whites and sprinkle with sugar. Bake at 350 degrees for about 25 minutes.

Orange Bread

Peelings from 2 oranges
Sugar
1 c. milk
1 egg, beaten
2 T. butter, melted
4 c. flour, sifted
Pinch of salt
4 t. baking powder

Slice orange peels into thin shreds. Put in a saucepan, cover with water, boil until tender. Measure, and add the same amount of sugar as you have peel and juice. Boil again until syrup is nearly all boiled away. When partly cool, add milk, beaten egg, melted butter, flour, salt and baking powder. Let stand 25 minutes. Bake at 325 degrees for 1 hour.

Banana Nut Bread

2 c. flour
1/2 t. baking soda
1/2 t. salt
2 t. baking powder
1/2 c. nutmeats, chopped
1/2 c. wheat bran
1/4 c. shortening
1/2 c. sugar
2 eggs
2 T. thick sour cream
1 1/2 c. mashed bananas

Sift together the flour, baking soda, salt and baking powder; stir in nut meats and wheat bran. Cream the shortening and sugar and add the eggs one at a time, mixing thoroughly after each one. Mix sour cream with banana; add to sugar mixture alternately with flour. Pour batter into a well greased loaf pan and bake at 350 degrees for about 1 1/4 hours. This bread is better if you wait till the second day before slicing it. Delicious with butter or plain cream cheese.

Chocolate Muffins

2 T. butter
1 c. sugar
2 eggs, separated
1 1/2 c. flour
1/2 c. coffee
2 t. cocoa
1 1/2 t. baking powder
1/2 t. vanilla

Cream together the butter and sugar. Beat egg whites until stiff; beat egg yolks until creamy. Add to sugar the egg yolks, then beat well. Add flour, coffee, cocoa, baking powder and vanilla and mix till well blended. Fold in egg whites. Put into greased muffin tins and bake about 20 minutes in a moderate over. You may use more cocoa if you like.

Graham Bread

3 c. graham flour
2 c. sweet milk
1/2 c. molasses
1 t. salt

Thoroughly mix together all ingredients. Pour into greased loaf pan and bake at 350 degrees for 45-50 minutes. Makes one loaf.

Norwegian Christmas Bread

2 c milk, scalded
1 yeast cake
Flour
1/2 c. sugar
1/2 c. butter, melted
Pinch of cardamom
1 c. raisins
3/4 c. citron, chopped
1 t. salt

Let milk cool; add yeast and enough flour to make a sponge, about 1-2 cups. Put in a warm place and let raise good, about an hour. Then add to it sugar, butter, cardamom, raisins, citron and salt. Mix well. Gradually add enough flour to knead into a stiff dough. Let raise again good (another hour) and then make into 2 round loaves. Let raise again; bake at 350 degrees for about 50 minutes. A raised nut bread can be made with this recipe by omitting the raisins and citron and adding 1 1/2 c. chopped walnuts.

Boston Brown Bread

1/2 c. corn meal
1 c. white flour
1/2 c. graham flour
1/2 c. molasses
1/2 c. raisins
1/2 c. nuts
1 1/2 c. sour milk
2 t. baking soda
A pinch of salt

Sift together the flours. Beat together the molasses, raisins, nuts, sour milk and baking soda. Add a pinch of salt; stir in flours. Turn into greased pans; let stand one hour. Bake about an hour in a moderate oven. Turn upside down to cool.

Elizabeth Arden beauty products were as popular as ever. In spite of the hard times, women still wanted to look their best.

Soft Ginger Bread

1/2 c. sugar
1 c. molasses
1/2 c. butter
1 t. ginger
1 t. cloves
1 t. cinnamon
2 t. baking soda
    dissolved in
1 c. boiling water
2 1/2 c. flour
2 eggs, well-beaten

Cream together the sugar, molasses and butter. Add spices and mix well. Pour in water with baking soda in it and mix. Gradually beat in flour, add the eggs the last thing. Bake in greased pan in a 350 degree oven for about an hour or until done.

Quick Graham Rolls

2 c. graham flour
1/2 t. salt
4 t. baking powder
2 T. fat
About 3/4 c. milk
Soft butter

Sift together the dry ingredients. Rub in the fat, add milk and mix to a smooth dough. Turn onto a floured board; divide dough into small portions and form into rolls the size and thickness of 2 fingers. Brush with soft butter; bake at 425 degrees, till brown.

Potato Biscuits

1 good-sized potato
1 1/2 c. flour
4 t. baking powder
1/2 t. salt
1/4 c. shortening
1 egg
About 1 c. milk

Boil and mash potato till it's free from lumps. Sift flour, salt and baking powder. Add potatoes and rub in shortening. Mix to a light dough with the egg and milk, roll out a little thinner than ordinary biscuit; bake in a hot oven (425 degrees) for 10-15 minutes until brown. Serve as soon as they are done.

Cream Muffins

1 1/2 c. flour
1/2 t. salt
1 T. baking powder
2 eggs, separated
1/4 c. shortening, melted
2/3 c. thin cream

Sift together the flour, salt and baking powder; ad the yolks of the eggs, melted shortening and cream, and beat well. Last of all, beat the egg whites until stiff and fold them into the batter. Put into well greased muffin pans and bake at 350 degrees for about 20 minutes.

Bran Muffins

Butter the size
   of an egg
2 T. sugar
1 egg, beaten
1/2 t. salt
2 c. buttermilk
2 c. flour
2 c. bran
1 t. baking soda

Cream together the butter and sugar; add salt and egg and beat well. Mix in buttermilk. Sift together the flour, add to batter. Stir in bran and baking soda. Bake in well greased muffin tins at 350 degrees for about 25 minutes. These are good for the digestion and they taste good too. Serve with butter.

Baking Powder Coffee Cake

1 1/2 c. flour
1/2 c. sugar
2 t. baking powder
1/2 t. salt
3 T. shortening
1 egg, beaten
1/2 c. milk
Melted butter
Streusel crumbs (see below)

Sift together the dry ingredients. Work shortening in with finger- tips or 2 knives. Stir in egg and milk; press lightly into greased cake pan. Pour melted butter over top, sprinkle with streusel crumbs and bake in a 400 degree oven for about half an hour. Cut into wedges and serve warm. Have the coffee all ready.

Streusel Crumbs

2 T. butter
2 T. sugar
1/4 c. flour
1/4 c. dry cake crumbs
1/2 t. cinnamon

Cream butter and sugar; add flour, finely ground cake crumbs (you can use bread crumbs if you don't have any cake crumbs) and cinnamon. Mix till crumbly and sprinkle on top of dough.

Banana Bread

1/2 c. shortening
1 c. sugar
2 eggs, beaten
3 bananas, ripe!
1 t. baking soda
2 c. flour
1/4 t. salt
4 t. sour milk

Cream shortening; add sugar and beat well. Add beaten eggs and mashed bananas. Sift flour, salt and baking soda; add alternately with sour milk and beat until smooth. Bake in a greased pan at 350 degrees for about 1 hour, or until done. Cool well before slicing. This is the best!

German Coffee Cake

3/8 c. milk
2 T. sugar
1 1/2 T. fat
1/2 t. salt
1/2 cake yeast (1 t.)
2 T. warm water
1 small egg, beaten
1 3/4 c. flour
Melted butter

Scald milk; pour over sugar, fat and salt in a bowl, cool. Soften yeast in warm water, add egg and mix. Add to milk mixture. Add about half the flour and beat well. Mix in rest of flour. Roll out 1/2" thick and place in well greased cake pan. Let rise until double. Prick top with a fork; brush with melted butter. Put streusel crumbs on top. Let rise for 1/2 hour; bake at 400 degrees for about 20 minutes.

Corn Bread

2 eggs
1/2 t. salt
2 c. milk
3 T. sugar
3/4 c. flour
4 t. baking powder
Yellow corn meal
    to form a batter

Beat the eggs well, add the salt, milk and sugar. Stir in the flour and baking powder; blend in enough corn meal to form a soft batter. The exact amount of corn meal can not be given - usually about 2 c. will be fine. Bake in shallow, well greased pans in a moderate oven about half an hour.

Southern Egg Bread

2 c. white corn meal
1 t. salt
1 T. baking powder
3 eggs
1 T. fat, melted
1 1/2 c. milk
1 c. cold, boiled rice

Sift together the corn meal, salt and baking powder. Beat the eggs well and add to corn meal; add melted fat, milk and rice. Beat thoroughly. Pour into a shallow, well greased pan and bake about half an hour in a hot oven - about 425 degrees.

Baking Powder Bread

2 c. fine whole wheat flour
4 t. baking powder
About 1 c. milk
2 t. sugar
1 t. salt

Sift together, twice, the dry ingredients; place in a large bowl and mix in the milk. When smooth, turn into a greased pan. Cover with another pan, inverted, and let stand 5-10 minutes. Bake about 45 minutes in an oven that's not too hot.

Oatmeal Sticks

3 c. flour
1/2 t. salt
1 T. sugar
1/4 c. shortening
1 1/4 c. milk, scalded
1/2 c. oatmeal
    or rolled oats
4 t. baking powder

Sift together the flour, salt, sugar and baking powder; rub in the shortening. Pour the hot milk over the oatmeal; cook, mix with other ingredients, working with your hands until dough is smooth. Roll into sticks about the length and thickness of a lead pencil. Bake about 10 minutes in a rather hot over, about 400 degrees.

Brown Bread

1 1/2 c. graham flour
1/2 c. white flour
1/2 t. salt
1 t. baking soda
1/2 c. sugar
1 c. sour milk

Sift the flour, salt and baking soda twice. Add the sugar and milk and mix to a batter. Pour into a well greased pan and bake in a slow oven (325 degrees) for about 40 minutes.

Whole Wheat Biscuits

2 c. whole wheat flour
4 t. baking powder
1 small egg
1/2 t. salt
2 T. shortening
About 1 c. milk

Sift flour, salt and baking powder together. Rub in shortening; add egg and milk and mix to a light dough. Roll out on a floured board, cut into biscuits and bake about 15 minutes in a hot oven, about 425 degrees.

Hot Cross Buns

1 1/2 c. milk
1/4 c. shortening
6 T. sugar
1/2 yeast cake (1 t.)
1 t. sugar
1 egg
2/3 c. currants and
    raisins, mixed
1 qt. flour
1/2 t. salt
1 t. cinnamon

Scald milk, shortening and sugar; cool to lukewarm. Mash yeast with sugar, add to milk. Add egg, currants and raisins. Sift flour, salt and cinnamon; add to mixture. Knead till smooth and elastic, as for bread; let rise in a warm place free from drafts, till very light. Divide into rounds a little larger than biscuits; work till smooth. Place on greased baking pan a little ways apart. Let rise again till light. With a sharp knife, mark a cross on each bun. Bake in a 350 degree oven until nearly done. Brush each bun with some milk, sprinkle with sugar, and return to oven for a moment or two until fully baked. Traditionally, these are made during Lent, but they are good anytime.

Poetry Biscuits

Two cups Indian, one cup wheat,
One cup sour milk, one cup sweet,
One cup good eggs that you can eat.
One-half cup molasses, too,
One-half cup sugar and thereto,
Salt and soda, each a spoon,
Mix up quickly and bake it soon.

Steamed Brown Bread

1 1/2 c. graham flour
3/4 c. yellow corn meal
4 t. baking powder
1/2 t. salt
1/4 c. molasses
1/2 c. raisins
1 egg
1 c. + 6 T. milk

Sift together the dry ingredients. Beat the egg, add milk and add to flour mixture. Add raisins and molasses. Have ready well greased tins with tightly fitting lids; steam 3 hours. The loaves may be placed in the oven for a few minutes after steaming, if a dry crust is desired.

Pies, Cakes & Pastries

"No soil upon earth is so dear to our eyes
As the soil we first stirred in terrestrial pies.
She may dress in silk, she may dress in satin,
She may know the language, Greek and Latin,
May know fine art, may love and sigh,
But she is no good if she can't make pie." - O. W. Holmes

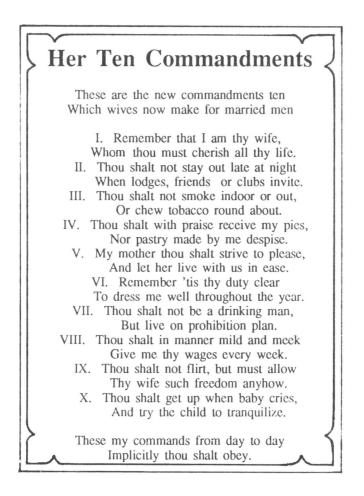

Her Ten Commandments

These are the new commandments ten
Which wives now make for married men

I. Remember that I am thy wife,
Whom thou must cherish all thy life.
II. Thou shalt not stay out late at night
When lodges, friends or clubs invite.
III. Thou shalt not smoke indoor or out,
Or chew tobacco round about.
IV. Thou shalt with praise receive my pies,
Nor pastry made by me despise.
V. My mother thou shalt strive to please,
And let her live with us in ease.
VI. Remember 'tis thy duty clear
To dress me well throughout the year.
VII. Thou shalt not be a drinking man,
But live on prohibition plan.
VIII. Thou shalt in manner mild and meek
Give me thy wages every week.
IX. Thou shalt not flirt, but must allow
Thy wife such freedom anyhow.
X. Thou shalt get up when baby cries,
And try the child to tranquilize.

These my commands from day to day
Implicitly thou shalt obey.

These Commandments are from Grandma Signe's recipe book.

Pie Crust

4 T. boiling water
4 T. lard
1 1/4 c. flour
1 t. baking powder
Pinch of salt

Melt lard in hot water. Mix together the flour, baking powder and salt and stir this into the liquid. Place in the ice box until cold. Roll out thin and line tin.

American women enjoyed wearing hats. Hats were very popular during the 30's, perhaps a relatively inexpensive frill that helped them feel good.

Cream Puffs

1/2 c. butter
4 eggs
1 c. boiling
1 c. flour

Put butter and water in a saucepan and place on front of range. As soon as it begins to boil, add the flour all at once, and stir briskly until mixture leaves the side of the pan. Remove from fire, add one unbeaten egg. Beat, add another, beat, and so on until the four have been added. Drop by spoonfuls into a buttered pan, two inches apart. Bake in a moderate oven about 30 minutes. With a sharp knife make a cut and fill with cream.

Cream filling:
3/4 c. whipping cream
1/4 c. sugar
1 egg white, beaten
1/2 t. vanilla

To make the cream filling; set medium sized bowl in pan of crushed ice and water. Place cream in bowl and beat until stiff. Whip up well, that air bubbles may not be too large. Add sugar, egg white and vanilla. Fill puffs and keep cool.

Popovers

7/8 c. milk
1 c. flour
2 eggs
1/2 t. fat, melted
1/4 t. salt

Mix flour and salt and 1/2 the milk. Beat until smooth. Add well beaten eggs and rest of milk and fat. Bake in hot oven (450 degrees) about 35 minutes in greased gem tins.

How to Render Lard

Grind pork fat or chop into small pieces. Put into large roasting pan and bake most of the day in a slow oven. Squash fat occasionally with a potato masher. Let it cool a bit. Carefully strain through cheesecloth and then pour fat into jars. Cover and store in a cool place or better yet in the ice box. Save the browned cracklings and use for flavoring as you would bacon.

Pie Crust

3 c. flour
1 c. lard
3 T. lemon juice
1 T. cold water
1 egg, beaten
1 t. salt

Cut flour and lard together with pastry blender or 2 table knives. Gently add lemon juice, water, egg and salt. Mix until just blended. Roll out and line pie tin. The less you handle the dough, the more tender it will be.

Plain Pastry

1 1/2 c. flour
1/2 c. lard
1 t. salt
1/2 t. baking powder
4 T. cold water

Sift together dry ingredients. Cut in lard. Add water a little at a time until dough holds together. Roll out on lightly floured board. Makes 2 crusts.

Mom's Rhubarb Pie

3 c. rhubarb
1 c. sugar
2 eggs
1/2 t. salt

Chop rhubarb and put into pie shell. Mix well the sugar, eggs and salt. Pour over rhubarb and bake in 350 degree oven till bubbly.

Grama's Good Pie Crust

1 1/2 c. flour, sifted
1/4 t. baking powder
1/2-1 t. salt
2/3 c. lard or shortening
3 T. sugar, if desired
About 1/3 c. cold water

Sift together dry ingredients. Add fat and cut with two knives or pastry blender until mealy. Stir in water until pastry leaves the sides of the bowl. Divide into 2 balls. Roll out one to fit pie tin, use the other for the top of the pie.

Chiffon Pie

3 eggs, separated
1 c. sugar, divided
1 lemon, grated
    & squeezed
A small piece
    of butter

Beat whites of eggs very stiff. Gradually add 1/2 of the sugar. Then in a saucepan, beat up the 3 yolks, add the other 1/2 c. sugar, lemon juice, rind and butter and cook until thick. (Stirring constantly.) Add the beaten white mixture. Put into crust and bake until set. Brown under fire, or broiler.

Pie Crust Supreme

1 1/2 c. flour
1/2 t. salt
1/4 t. baking powder
1/2 c. lard
2 T. butter
2 T. egg, beaten
3 T. ice water
1/2 t. vinegar

Combine flour, salt, baking powder, lard and butter and blend with a pastry blender. Mix egg, ice water and vinegar. Add to dry mixture a little at a time until all flour is moistened. You may not need all the liquid. Makes enough dough for a two crust pie.

Mrs. Storer's Lemon Meringue Pie

1 c. sugar
1 c. water
1 lemon, grated
   & squeezed
2 egg yolks
1 heaping T. corn starch
   in 1/2 c. water

Meringue
2 egg whites
1/4 t. cream of
   tartar
3 T. sugar
1/2 t. vanilla

Put sugar and water in a pan to boil. Add the lemon juice, rind and egg yolks. Stir cornstarch mixture into syrup and boil until it's clear. Take off fire and stir occasionally until mixture is cool. Pour into a baked pie shell. Beat the egg whites until they are frothy. Add cream of tartar and beat again until they stiff but not dry. Beat in sugar 1/2 t. at a time. Add vanilla. Cover lemon mixture with meringue. Bake about 15 minutes in a 350 degree oven. Cool in a warm place away from drafts.

Pastry Trimmin's Treats

Pastry trimmings
Sugar
Cinnamon

Place assorted shapes of trimmings from your pie on a cookie tin. Sprinkle with sugar and cinnamon and bake about 15 minutes. Serve warm. The kids will eat these all up in a hurry, so get yours first!

Pastry Crackers

Pastry trimmings
Grated cheese
   OR
Chopped nuts

Roll trimmings into a rectangle. Sprinkle with cheese or nuts, fold ends to center. Sprinkle again, fold again. Roll out to 1/4" thick. Cut into strips, twist them, and bake in a hot oven.

Mama's Pumpkin Pie

1 c. pumpkin, cooked
1 c. sugar
2 eggs
1/2 t. salt
1 t. ginger
1 t. cinnamon
1 pt. milk

Beat eggs well. Add sugar, pumpkin, salt and spices. Mix until well blended. Add milk and beat again. Pour into pie crust (unbaked) and bake in a hot oven for about 10 minutes. Then reduce the heat to about 325 degrees bake for about 50 minutes more. You can make this with leftover squash and nobody will know the difference.

You can get by with just about anything for supper if you have pie for dessert!

How to Cook Pumpkin for Pie

Slice, peel and then cut pumpkin (or squash) into small pieces. Put into a saucepan with a little water, cover and simmer until it's tender. Drain, let cool, and force through a strainer, or mash with a potato masher.

Banana Cream Pie

3 eggs
3/4 c. sugar
1 1/2 c. milk
2 T. cornstarch
1 t. vanilla
A few bananas

Bake pie crust; cool. Line with sliced bananas. Put milk in saucepan and let come to a boil. Beat eggs, add sugar, cornstarch and a little of the hot milk. Pour this into boiling milk, stirring constantly with a whisk. When thick enough, remove from fire. Add vanilla. Cool a little, and pour over bananas in pie crust.

Buttermilk Spice Doughnuts

1 c. sugar
2 eggs, well beaten
1/4 c. soft shortening
4 c. flour
2 t. baking powder
1 t. baking soda
1/2 t. salt
1/4 t. nutmeg
1 c. buttermilk

Gradually add sugar to eggs, beating well after each addition. Beat in shortening. Sift together dry ingredients. Add to sugar mixture alternately with buttermilk, mixing well after each addition. Chill dough. Turn dough onto floured pastry cloth or board. Knead 3-4 times to form a ball. Cut in half. Roll each half about 1/3" thick and cut with a sharp cutter. Fry in hot fat.

Doughnuts

3 eggs
1 1/2 c. sugar
1 c. sweet milk
1/2 t. salt
3 T. butter, melted
2 t. cream of tartar
1 t. baking soda
Dash nutmeg
Grated lemon peel
Flour

Beat eggs well and add sugar, mixing well. Add milk, salt, butter, cream of tartar and baking soda. Beat well. Flavor with nutmeg and lemon. Add enough flour to make a soft dough. Roll out about 1/2" thick and cut with a double cutter, or two different sized biscuit cutters. Let doughnuts dry for about 10 minutes before frying hot fat. Makes about 3 dozen. These are even better when sprinkled with a little powdered sugar.

Devil's Food Cake

2 c. sugar
1/2 c. shortening
   OR lard
2 eggs
Pinch of salt
1/2 c. cocoa
1/2 c. boiling water
1 t. baking soda
1 c. sour milk
1 t. vanilla
2 1/2 c. flour

Dissolve baking soda in water. Then mix together all ingredients in the order given. Grease and flour pans, bake in a 375 degree oven for 45-50 minutes.

Rich Raisin Cake

1 lb. raisins
Water
1 c. sugar
Vinegar
Cornstarch
3/4 c. lard
1 3/4 c. oatmeal
1 3/4 c. flour
1 t. baking soda
Pinch of salt
1 c. brown sugar

Cook raisins till soft in water. Add 1 c. sugar or enough to sweeten. Add a little vinegar to taste, and thicken with cornstarch mixed with a little water to make a paste. Mix shortening, baking soda, salt, brown sugar and flour like you do for pie crust. Grease pan and put crumbs in bottom. Pour on raisin mixture, put rest of crumbs on top. Bake in a quick oven. Serve with ice cream or whipped cream.

Cake - Marion Partridge

1/2 c. butter
3/4 c. sugar
2 eggs, beaten
1/2 c. milk
1 t. vanilla
1 1/2 c. flour
2 t. baking powder

Beat butter and sugar together. Add eggs and beat well. Put vanilla into milk and add to mixture. Gradually beat in flour and baking powder, mix till smooth. Pour into greased and floured pan and bake in a moderate oven.

Norman Rockwell was busy pleasing the public with his ever-popular paintings.

Good Cake Without Frosting

3 c. flour
1/2 t. grd. cloves
1/2 t. salt
1 c. shortening
  OR lard
1/2 t. cinnamon
1/2 t. nutmeg
2 c. brown sugar

Egg mixture
1 c. sour milk
1 t. baking soda
2 eggs, beaten

Mix together flour, cloves, salt, shortening, cinnamon, nutmeg and brown sugar. Take out 2/3 c. of mixture for topping. To rest of mixture, add milk, baking soda and eggs. Beat well. Pour batter into greased pan; put egg mixture on top of cake and bake in a slow oven till done.

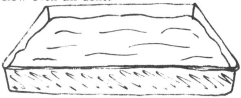

Red Devil's Food Cake

1/2 c. fat
1 c. sugar
2 eggs
1/2 c. sour milk
1 t. vanilla
2 sqs. chocolate
1/2 c. boiling water
1 1/2 c. flour
1 t. baking soda
1 t. baking powder
1/4 t. salt

Cream fat and sugar. Add eggs, milk (or buttermilk or cold coffee) and vanilla. Melt chocolate in boiling water; add to mixture. Beat for two minutes. Add other ingredients. Beat one minute. (This is a thin batter but will thicken when baked.) Pour into a shallow pan lined with wax paper. Bake 30 minutes in a moderate oven.

Aunt Annie's Sponge Cake

4 eggs
1 c. sugar
4 T. cold water
1 c. flour
1 T. cornstarch
1 t. baking powder
1 t. vanilla

Separate eggs. Beat egg yolks with sugar. Add water and mix well. Stir in flour, cornstarch, baking powder and vanilla and stir till well blended. Beat egg whites with a clean beater until stiff. Gently fold egg whites into batter. Bake in a moderate oven. Very good!

From Mrs. McGrath: "I made such a rotten cake that Bill wouldn't talk to me for a week. (The fact is he got sick and couldn't talk at all for a week.)"

Brown Sugar Cake

1 c. lard
2 c. brown sugar
4 egg yolks
2 egg whites
1 c. sour milk
2 3/4 c. flour
1/2 t. salt
1 t. cinnamon
1 t. ground cloves
1 t. allspice
1 t. baking powder
1 t. baking soda

Frosting
2 egg whites
1 c. brown sugar

Beat together lard and brown sugar until creamy. Beat in the 4 egg yolks and 2 egg whites. Add milk. Stir in flour and remaining dry ingredients. Pour into greased tin. Then beat the other 2 egg whites with brown sugar. Spread over cake dough and bake all in a moderate oven for about 40 minutes.

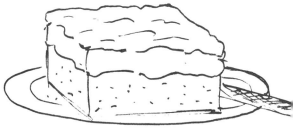

Devil's Food Cake

1 c. chocolate, grated
1/2 c. sugar
1/2 c. sweet milk
1 t. vanilla
1 c. sugar
1/2 c. butter
2 eggs
1/2 c. sweet milk
2 c. flour
1 t. baking soda

In top of double boiler, dissolve first four ingredients: chocolate, sugar, milk and vanilla. Set aside to cool. Then beat together the other sugar and butter. Add eggs and milk and mix well. Add flour and baking soda. Stir cooled chocolate mixture into cake batter. Pour into greased pan and bake in moderate oven till done.

Devil's Food Cake

1 c. sugar
3/4 c. butter
3 eggs
3 bars Baker's chocolate
1 c. milk
2 c. flour
3 heaping t. baking powder
1 t. flavoring

In top of double boiler, melt chocolate and butter. Take off heat, beat in sugar. Add eggs and milk. Stir in flour, baking powder and flavoring. Put into greased pan and bake in a 350 degree oven.

Mable's Cake

1 c. sugar
1 c. raisins
1 c. water
1/2 c. lard
1 t. baking soda
2 c. flour
1/2 t. salt
1 t. cinnamon
1 t. ground cloves
1 t. nutmeg

In a medium sized saucepan, mix together sugar, raisins, water and lard. Bring to a boil and stir in baking soda. Cool and add flour, salt and spices. Mix well. Bake in moderate oven.

Aunt Dodie's Butter Cream Cake

1/2 c. butter
1 1/2 c. sugar
1 c. milk
1 t. lemon extract
2 1/4 c. flour, sifted
2 1/2 t. baking powder
3 egg whites,
    well beaten

Cream together butter and sugar. Add milk a little at a time. Add lemon. Gradually beat in flour and baking soda. Carefully fold in beaten egg whites. Turn into greased and floured pan and bake in a moderate oven until done.

Fruit Cake

2 c. sugar
1 c. butter
    OR lard
1 c. milk
    OR coffee
4 eggs
3 1/2 c. flour
3 t. baking powder
1/2 t. salt
1 t. cinnamon
1 t. vanilla
A little clove
A little allspice
1 pt. butternut meats
1 pt. raisins
    OR currants
1/2 lb. figs
1/2 lb. dates
A little citron

Put all the fruits and nuts into a bowl. Stir in 1/2 c. of the flour; set aside. Cream together the sugar and butter. Add eggs and milk and beat well. Stir in flour and spices till mixed. Stir in fruits and nuts. Bake in greased tins 275 degrees for 1 1/2 hours. This recipe makes two loaves. From Mrs. Kenyon.

Lifebuoy Health Soap promised to end "that common yet never forgiven fault, B.O."

Mrs. Knowles' Radio Cake

1 1/2 c. sugar
1/2 c. butter
3 eggs, beaten good
2 c. flour
1 t. baking soda
1 t. baking powder
1 t. cinnamon
1 t. allspice
1 t. nutmeg
1 c. sour milk

Beat together sugar and butter until creamy. Beat in eggs. Sift flour, then measure. Sift all dry ingredients together. Pour about 1/3 of the milk into the sugar mixture and mix well. Then put about 1/3 of the dry mixture in and beat well again. Continue alternating liquid and dry. Add a cupful of dates or nuts if desired. Bake in a moderate oven till it tests done.

Maureen's Chocolate Cake

2 c. sugar
1/2 c. shortening
2 eggs
1 c. sour milk
2 t. baking soda
2 t. vanilla
2 1/2 c. flour
1/2 c. cocoa
1 c. boiling water

Cream sugar and shortening, add eggs, cream again. Add remaining ingredients, one at a time, in order given. Pour into a greased and floured large pan or into layer pans. Bake in a moderate oven for 40-45 minutes.

Joe's Soft Ginger Cake

1/2 c. shortening
    (Crisco)
2/3 c. sugar
1 t. salt
1/2 c. molasses
1 1/2 t. baking soda in
    1 c. boiling water
2 1/2 c. flour
1 t. cinnamon
1/2 t. ginger
1/2 t. ground cloves
2 eggs, beaten

Mix together shortening, sugar, salt and molasses. Add the soda-in-water while hot. Mix and add the flour. Mix in spices. Finally mix in the beaten eggs. Pour into greased pan and bake in moderate (350 degree) oven for 30 minutes.

Even when the Depression was at its worst, people still managed to buy radios. They were a great source of entertainment, and since many people were not working as much, or at all, they had more free time to listen.

Aunt Dodie's Eggless Cake

1 c. sugar
1/2 c. lard
1 c. sweet milk
1 t. vanilla
1/2 t. ground cloves
1/2 t. cinnamon
1 t. salt
1 scant t. cream
    of tartar
1 scant t. baking soda
2 c. flour

Cream sugar and lard. Add milk and vanilla. Add cloves, cinnamon and salt. Mix together the cream of tartar, baking soda and flour. Beat this into batter, a little at a time. Pour into a greased tin, bake in a moderate oven until done. This is good with a little cream poured over each serving.

Quick Cake

1/3 c. butter, soft
1 1/3 c. brown sugar
2 eggs
1/2 c. milk
1 3/4 c. flour
3 t. baking powder
1/2 t. salt
1 t. cinnamon
1/2 lb. dates

Beat well butter and sugar. Add eggs and milk. Add remaining ingredients and beat everything together. Beat for three minutes. Bake 45-50 minutes in a moderate oven. From Mrs. Louie Johnson.

Novel Layer Cake

First Layer
1/2 c. shortening
1 c. sugar
2 eggs, beaten
1/2 t. vanilla
3/4 t. salt
1 1/2 c. pastry flour

Cream shortening and sugar. Add eggs and vanilla. Last, sift flour and salt and mix together well. Spread even in greased pan.

Second Layer
1 c. brown sugar
1 egg white
1/2 t. vanilla
3/4 c. nuts, chopped
1 T. cocoa

Beat egg white well and fold in sugar and cocoa. Add vanilla and stir gently. Spread over first layer in pan. Sprinkle with walnuts. Bake in a 350 degree oven for about 30 minutes. From Mrs. Neiman.

Gold Cake

1 2/3 c. flour
1 t. baking powder
1/2 t. salt
10 egg yolks
1/2 c. boiling water
1 c. sugar

Mix together flour, baking powder and salt; sift three times. Beat the egg yolks a little. Add the boiling water a little at a time. Add the sugar slowly. Beat for 10 minutes. By hand, carefully fold in sifted flour mixture. Bake at 350 degrees for 1 hour.

Mrs. Babich's Cake

2 c. cake flour
1/2 c. butter OR Crisco
1 1/4 c. sugar
1 t. salt (or less)
1/2 c. milk
3 t. baking powder
2 eggs
1/3 c. more milk
1 t. vanilla

Sift flour, then measure. Cream butter and add flour, sugar, salt and milk. Beat this two minutes. Gradually add remaining ingredients and beat two minutes longer. Pour into a greased pan. Put in a moderate oven. Bakes in 30-35 minutes. Good!

Clara's Chocolate Cake

1 1/2 c. sugar
1/2 c. shortening OR lard
3 eggs
2 sqs. chocolate
2 T. boiling water
3/4 c. sour milk
1 t. baking soda
2 c. flour
1/2 t. salt
2 t. flavoring (vanilla)

Melt chocolate in boiling water. Cool. Dissolve baking soda in milk. Meantime, beat together sugar and shortening. Add chocolate. Add eggs one at a time and beat well. Stir in milk. Add flour, salt and flavoring. Pour into greased and floured pans and bake in a moderate oven for about 40-50 minutes.

Agnes Johnson's Sugarless Cake

1/2 c. butter
1 c. light corn syrup
2 eggs, separated
1/2 c. milk
2 1/4 c. cake flour
2 1/4 t. baking powder
1/2 t. salt

Cream butter. Add syrup gradually, then add egg yolks. Sift flour and baking powder and add alternately with milk. Beat egg whites stiff but not dry. Pour into pan and bake 45 minutes at 350 degrees. Serve with whipping cream. Very good.

Sponge Cake

6 eggs, separated
1 1/2 c. sugar
1/2 c. water
1/4 t. salt
1 c. flour
3/4 t. cream of tartar

Beat egg whites with rotary beater until stiff. Put sugar and water in a saucepan and boil until it threads. Then beat into egg whites until cold. Beat yolks good, until light and foamy. Beat cold whites into yolks. Mix together the flour, salt and cream of tartar. Fold carefully into egg mixture by hand and put into tins. Bake in 275 degree oven 45 minutes, then 300 degrees until nearly done, and then 5 minutes at 325 degrees. This is kind of complicated, but the results are good.

Maple Sugar Filling & Frosting

1 lb. maple sugar
Water
1/2 c. cream
1 T. butter
1 t. vanilla

Break maple sugar into small pieces; cover with enough water to thoroughly dissolve and boil until it waxes hard. Take off heat and beat till nearly cold. Add cream and butter. Put on fire again and cook till the right consistency. Beat till cool and add vanilla.

Frosting

1 T. butter
1 egg yolk
1 T. cocoa
1 T. warm, black coffee
2 c. powdered sugar

Mix butter and egg yolk well. Beat in cocoa and coffee. Gradually add sugar. Spread on cooled cake. Easy and tasty.

Nut Caramel Icing

1 1/4 c. brown sugar
1/3 c. water
1/4 c. sugar
2 egg whites,
  beaten stiff
1 t. vanilla
1/4 c. English walnuts,
  broken into pieces

Boil sugars and water without stirring until syrup will thread when dropped from tip of spoon. Pour gradually, while beating constantly, on egg whites and continue beating until nearly cool. Set pan containing mixture into pan of boiling water and cook over flame, stirring constantly until mixture becomes granular around edge of pan. Remove from pan of water and beat, using a spoon, until mixture will hold its shape. Add nuts and vanilla. Spread.

1933: *"Gold Diggers of 1933" was at "the show" and starred Dick Powell, Joan Blondell and Warren Williams.*

Boiled Chocolate Frosting

2 oz. chocolate
1/2 c. milk
2 egg whites
Vanilla
Powdered sugar

In double boiler, boil chocolate and cream; cool, add vanilla. Beat egg whites to a stiff froth; add the sugar until stiff enough to cut. Combine the two mixtures, beat and spread.

Mocha Frosting

1 c. powdered sugar
1 t. cocoa
2 T. butter
1/4 t. vanilla
2 T. cold, strong coffee

Cream butter. Add sugar and cocoa gradually. Add vanilla, then coffee, gradually until mixture is smooth, creamy and thick enough to spread.

Boiled Icing

1 c. sugar
1/3 c. water
1/4 t. cream of tartar
1 t. flavoring
1 large egg white

Beat egg white until frothy, add cream of tartar. Beat until stiff and dry. Cook sugar and water until it has reached the honey stage, or drops heavily from spoon. Add 5 T. slowly to egg, beating in well. Then cook remainder of syrup until it threads and pour over egg, beating thoroughly. Add flavoring and beat until cool.

Icing for White Cake

1 1/2 c. sugar
1 c. water
2 egg whites
1/2 c. pineapple, chopped

Boil sugar and water until it threads well; pour over egg whites well beaten, beating all the time. When partly cool, add pineapple.

Frosting

2 egg whites
Powdered sugar
1 orange, juice & rind

Beat egg whites till stiff. Add enough powdered sugar to make it thick, add orange rind and juice.

Frosting

2 egg whites
3 T. water
1 c. sugar
1/2 t. cream of tartar

Put all ingredients in top of double boiler; be sure water is boiling. Beat for about four minutes. Very good. From Mrs. Fredrick.

Seven Minute Frosting

2 egg whites
1 1/2 c. sugar
1/4 t. cream of tartar
1/3 c. water

Over boiling water in double boiler, beat all ingredients until mixture stands in stiff peaks, about seven minutes. Don't make this on a humid hot day - it won't work.

Praline Frosting

1/3 c. brown sugar
1 t. flour
1/3 c. nuts, chopped
3 T. butter, melted
1 T. water

Mix together well and spread over warm cake. Place in moderate oven (350 degrees) for about 5 minutes. Will frost a small cake. For a large cake, double the recipe.

Icing

2 c. brown sugar
1/2 c. cream
1/2 c. maple syrup
Butter the size of a walnut

Mix all together in a saucepan. Let boil until it forms a soft ball in ice cold water. Beat until creamy. Spread on cake.

Caramel Frosting

2 c. brown sugar
1/2 c. cream
1 T. butter
1/3 t. vanilla

In a saucepan mix brown sugar, cream and butter. Boil until ball forms in ice cold water. Remove from fire and add vanilla. Beat until to right consistency to spread. From Mrs. Dalley.

Caramel Frosting

1 1/2 c. brown sugar
1/2 c. milk
1 T. butter
Vanilla
Nuts

Cook sugar and milk to boiling. Boil until a firm ball is formed when tested with cold water. Take off fire, cool and beat in butter and vanilla and nuts until thick enough to spread.

Crullers

1 t. baking soda in 4 T. milk
1/2 pt. flour (1 c.)
4 T. butter, melted
4 eggs
6 heaping T. sugar
Flour

Pour soda-in-milk into flour, add melted butter and stir to mix. Beat eggs with sugar; work them into the rest of the ingredients. Add enough flour to make a stiff dough that can be rolled out. Roll, cut and fry in hot lard; flavor with a little grated nutmeg.

Rhubarb Pie

1 c. flour
1 T. powdered sugar
1/2 c. butter
2 eggs, beaten
1 c. sugar
1/4 c. flour
1/2 t. salt
2 c. rhubarb

Cream together the flour, powdered sugar and butter. Pat it into the bottom of a pie tin. Bake at 350 degrees for about 15 minutes. Meanwhile, mix together the beaten eggs, sugar, flour and salt; beat until creamy. Stir in the rhubarb and pour this mixture into the cooled pie crust. Bake at 350 degrees for 45 minutes or until set. This is really good.

Johnny Cake

1 c. flour
1 t. salt
1 c. corn meal
3/4 t. baking soda
1 t. baking powder
2 eggs, beaten
1 1/2 c. sour milk
2 T. brown sugar
1/4 c. lard, melted

Sift together flour, salt, baking soda and baking powder. Beat the eggs well and add milk and melted lard and sugar. Stir together liquid and dry ingredients; gently fold in corn meal, stirring only until just mixed. Bake in a well greased pan at 425 degrees for about 25 minutes or until done.

Johnny Cake

2 T. melted cracklings or fat
2 eggs
1 t. salt
2 c. buttermilk
1 t. baking soda
2 c. corn meal

Beat eggs well and add salt, buttermilk and soda. Stir in corn meal and melted fat. Mix only to moisten; do not over beat. Pour into greased baking tins and bake at 400 degrees for 20-25 minutes.

According to legend, here's how Johnny Cake got its name: Back East women used to bake a corn meal cake that kept quite well. Men would take some along with them on their travels. Since New Englanders don't always pronounce the letter "R" unless it's at the end of a sentence, words like "journey cake" came to be pronounced "jou'ney cake." Say it fast - it's "Johnny Cake."

124

Cookies, Desserts & Puddings

She stood at the table with sugar and spice
And raisins and currants and everything nice,
And cut little round things as fast as she could,
Baked them and then they were cookies and good.

FRESH ·· FRAGRANT ···
these Sun-Maid Nectars

How you will enjoy cooking with seedless raisins

that add the flavor of grapes!

AS IF the juice
in the grape had
merely jelled—
they are so tender
and plump, so
rich in flavor.

Cup Custard

1 egg
1 T. sugar
A drop or two of
    flavoring or spice
Speck of salt
1/2 c. milk

Beat lightly together all ingredients. Pour into greased custard cups and cook slowly with cups set in pan of water until set. This doesn't make a lot, so you may want to double or even triple the recipe.

Caramel Custard

4 c. milk
5 eggs, slightly beaten
1/2 t. salt
1 t. vanilla
1 c. sugar

Scald milk. Melt sugar to a light brown syrup; add scalded milk and add this mixture to eggs. Pour into custard cups, place in pan of water and bake slowly in oven until firm. Try this one!

Whipped Cream Dessert

1 pt. whipping
    cream, beat stiff
1/2 c. pineapple, cubed
Few marshmallows,
    chopped fine
Few black walnuts, chopped

Mix all ingredients together and serve in dessert or parfait glasses. Serve with nut wafers. This delicious dessert is very fine and does not take long to prepare. Enough for 6 people - it's very rich.

Apple Pudding

4 lg. apples
2 eggs, beaten
1 c. sugar
2 T. flour
1 t. baking powder
Vanilla

Peel, core and cut apples fine. Mix together eggs, sugar, flour and baking powder. Stir in vanilla and apples. Bake in a moderate oven until it's firm.

Rhubarb Pudding

2 c. rhubarb
1 c. sugar
2 eggs
1/2 c. milk
1/4 c. flour
1/2 t. baking powder
Pinch of salt
A little grated lemon

Clean rhubarb and cut into small pieces. Mix together eggs and sugar. Add one at a time the remaining ingredients. Stir in rhubarb pieces. Pour into buttered cake pan and put little dabs of butter on top. Bake at 375 degrees for 30-35 minutes. This is good by itself or with a little whipped cream on top. Maybe some nuts.

Rice Pudding

1 qt. milk
1/2 c. rice
1 T. flour
1 egg
1/4 c. milk
Sugar
Salt

Put milk in the top of a double boiler. Add rice to cold milk and cook until the rice is tender. Beat together the flour, egg and milk. Stir this into the rice and cook until it thickens. Stir in a little salt and add sugar to taste. Serve hot or cold.

Caramel Pudding

2 c. brown sugar
3 small c. water
3 t. cornstarch
   (rounded)
1 c. walnuts, chopped
1 t. vanilla

Put sugar and water in a saucepan and bring to a boil. Dissolve cornstarch in a little cold water, add to syrup and boil about 5 minutes. Stir occasionally. Take from fire and add nuts and vanilla. Pour into small bowls, cool. Serve with whipped cream.

Rhubarb Dessert

1 1/2 c. rhubarb
1 c. sugar
1 egg
2 T. flour

Batter
1 c. flour
1/2 c. milk
Pinch of salt
2 T. butter
1 heaping t. baking powder

Wash rhubarb and cut into pieces. Mix together sugar, egg and flour. Add to rhubarb and put in a baking dish. Then make a batter of the flour, milk, salt, butter and baking powder. Put this batter on top of rhubarb mixture and bake until done. Serve with cream, either plain or whipped. This dish can be made with apples, too, if you don't have any rhubarb.

American Cornstarch Pudding

1/2 c. sugar
3 T. cornstarch
1/4 t. salt
2 c. milk
1 1/2 t. vanilla

Mix it all in a saucepan except for the milk and vanilla. Put on the fire and slowly add the milk while stirring constantly until thick enough. Add vanilla. Serves four people. (In later years, Jackie Kennedy served this at a state dinner, but then it was called "Blanc Mange." Would the guests have eaten it otherwise?)

1936: *The Boulder Dam (later called the Hoover Dam) was completed.*

128

Steamed Graham Pudding

1/2 t. baking soda
1 c. suet
1 c. molasses
1 c. milk
1 c. raisins
1/2 t. cinnamon
1/2 t. nutmeg
2 c. graham flour
English walnuts,
    chopped

Sauce for Pudding
1 c. sugar, pulverized
3/4 c. butter
1 T. boiling water
1 egg white

Dissolve baking soda in a little hot water. Beat suet until soft. Gradually add in molasses. Stir in remaining ingredients. To steam: grease well the insides of pudding molds or tins that have tight fitting lids, then sprinkle insides with sugar. Containers should be only 2/3 full. Place molds on a trivet in a heavy kettle containing an inch of water. Cover tightly. Steam over high heat at first, then over low heat for three hours total time. For sauce, mix all ingredients together, then beat very well until it's light and fluffy.

Caramel Cream Pudding

2 T. shortening
2 T. sugar
1 egg
1 c. flour
3/4 t. baking powder
1/4 t. salt
1/4 c. milk

Sauce
1 1/2 c. sour cream
3/4 c. sour milk
2 1/4 c. brown sugar
1/4 c. flour

Beat shortening and sugar together till creamy. Add egg and beat hard for about 2 minutes. Sift together flour, baking powder and salt. Add to creamed mixture alternately with the milk. Put dough in the bottom of a baking tin. For the sauce: Using an egg beater, mix together the sour cream, sour milk, sugar and flour. Pour the sauce over the dough and bake in a 350 degree oven for about 45 minutes. As this bakes, the sauce sinks to the bottom, and the dough comes to the top! Serve hot.

Aunt Annie's Icebox Cookies

1/2 c. lard
1/4 c. sugar
1/4 c. brown sugar
1 1/4 c. flour
1 egg
1/4 t. salt

Beat lard and sugars together until fluffy. Add egg, beat well. Add flour and salt, mix thoroughly. Chill in icebox several hours until firm. Slice with a sharp knife and put on baking sheet and bake in a moderate oven until light brown.

Plum Pudding

1 c. milk
1/2 lb. bread crumbs
1/2 lb. suet, chopped
1/2 lb. sugar
4 eggs, separated
1/2 lb. raisins, seeded
1/2 lb. currants
1/2 lb. figs, chopped
1/4 lb. citron, sliced
1/2 c. brandy
1 t. nutmeg
1/2 t. cinnamon
1/2 t. ground cloves
1/4 t. mace
1 t. salt
1 c. flour
1 t. baking powder, heaping
1 c. almonds,
    blanched & chopped

Scald milk and pour over crumbs. Beat suet until creamy and then add the sugar. Add beaten egg yolks and mix well. Add cooled milk-and-crumbs. Next add raisins, figs, currants, citron, nuts, salt and spices. Add brandy, flour and baking powder and lastly the well beaten egg whites. Pour into a buttered mold and steam 5-6 hours. This will make one large or two small ones.

Mrs. McGrath wrote: "Dorothy is sick and I feel guilty because she ate pretty much of the plum pudding I made the other day." Maybe a little of this is plumb enough.

Cookies

1 c. butter
2 c. flour
5 T. sugar
1 c. nutmeats
1 T. water
1/2 t. vanilla

Whip butter until soft. Add sugar and beat until fluffy. Mix in flour, water, vanilla and nuts. Shape into balls as large as a quarter. Place on cookie sheet and bake until lightly browned, about 10 minutes or so. From Aunt Minnie.

Mrs. Carl Peterson's Cookies

1 c. lard OR shortening
1 c. sugar
1/2 c. molasses
1 t. baking soda
1 t. ginger
1 egg
2 c. flour

Beat lard or shortening until it is soft. Add sugar, and beat again. Add egg, beat until it's fluffy. Put in molasses, baking soda and ginger and mix well. Stir in flour. Drop by spoonfuls on a baking sheet. Bake in a moderate oven about 10 minutes, or until golden brown. Grandma Signe wrote in her cookbook, next to this recipe, the single word, "Good."

Scalloped Rhubarb

4 c. soft bread crumbs
1/4 c. butter, melted
4 c. rhubarb, 1" pieces
2 c. sugar
A little cinnamon
A few lemon rind gratings
A few orange ring gratings

Fill a buttered baking dish, in layers, in order given. Cover tightly and bake in a moderate oven for about 30 minutes. You might want to serve this with some whipped cream or maybe just some regular cream to moisten it up a bit.

French Rice

2 c. milk
1 c. water
1 c. rice, washed
1 T. butter
1 t. salt
2 t. vanilla

Filling
Heavy cream, whipped
Sugar to sweeten
A few nuts, chopped

Put milk and water in a saucepan and heat. Put the rice into the double boiler and pour the hot liquid over it, adding the butter and salt. Heat the mass, then add the vanilla. When the rice has taken up all the liquid and is puffed up, arrange it in a ring on a plate and chill. When ready to serve, fill the center of ring with whipped cream mixture.

Bread Pudding

3 c. milk
2 c. fine bread crumbs
2 egg yolks
1 scant c. sugar
1 c. raisins OR 2 lg.
   apples sliced fine
1/2 t. salt
Butter
2 egg whites,
   beaten stiff
2 T. powdered sugar
Marshmallows

Scald milk and add bread crumbs. Let cool a little and add the egg yolks, sugar, raisins or apples and salt. Turn into pudding dish, put bits of butter on top, and bake. When done, top with meringue made of egg whites and powdered sugar. Dot with marshmallows cut in halves and return to oven and brown a little. Serve warm or cold. It's better made with apples unless you really like raisins.

1939: *Chocolate chips were first produced by Nestle, after being experimented with by Ruth Wakefield, the owner of the Toll House Inn, in the early thirties. She cut up a Nestle Semi-Sweet Chocolate bar into tiny pieces and added them to her cookie dough. She thought they'd melt, but they didn't. And thus, the Toll House Cookie was born. Mrs. Wakefield agreed to having Nestle put her recipe on the chocolate chip package, and the little pieces of ready-to-use chocolate were marketed.*

Delicious Cookies

3 egg whites
1 small c. sugar
1 c. nutmeats or
   1 c. coconut
Corn flakes

Beat egg whites until stiff. Fold in gently the sugar and nutmeats or coconut. Add enough corn flakes to stiffen the mixture. Drop from spoon onto buttered pan and brown in hot oven (425 degrees.) From Aunt Agnes.

Annetta's Cookies

2 c. brown sugar
A good 1/2 c. butter
3 eggs, beaten
2 T. hot water
1 t. vanilla
3 1/2 c. flour, sifted
1 t. baking soda
1 t. cinnamon
Pinch of salt
1 c. nuts, chopped

Cream together sugar and butter. Add eggs, water and vanilla. Beat well. Sift together flour, baking soda, cinnamon and salt. Add to mixture, and stir in nuts. Pat into wafers with fingers and bake in a hot oven for about 10 minutes.

Aunt Dodie's Cookies

1/2 c. sugar
1/2 c. butter
1 egg, well beaten
1 1/4 c. flour
1 t. baking powder
Pinch salt
1 lemon rind, grated
Walnut halves

Mix sugar and butter together until creamy. Beat in egg. Add flour, baking powder, salt and lemon rind. Mold into balls half the size of a walnut. Lay on a greased tin and press down with a fork dipped in flour. Place 1/2 walnut on each and bake in a moderate oven until browned.

Aunt Minnie's Oatmeal Cookies

1 c. lard OR
   shortening
1 1/2 c. brown sugar
1/2 c. sugar
2 eggs, beaten
1 t. vanilla
1 t. salt
1 t. baking soda
1 1/2 c. flour
3 c. oatmeal
1/2 c. nuts, chopped

Beat shortening and sugars well. Add eggs and vanilla and beat well again. Stir in remaining ingredients. Shape into a loaf. Chill overnight. In the morning, slice and bake 10 minutes in a 350 degree oven.

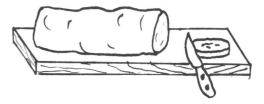

"Cookies"

1 c. shortening
1 c. brown sugar
2 eggs
1 c. milk
2 c. oatmeal
1 c. flour (add
    more if necessary)

Filling
1 c. sugar
1 c. water
1/2 lb. dates, ground

Beat together shortening and sugar. Add eggs - mix well. Mix in milk, and add the other ingredients. Roll out and cut in rounds with a biscuit cutter. Bake till light brown in 350 degree oven. After baked, put two together with filling. To make the filling; combine all and boil till thick, stirring once in a while. Cool a little and spread on cookies. From Elice.

Butter Cookies

1 c. butter
1/2 c. powdered sugar
1/4 t. salt
2 3/4 c. flour
1 t. vanilla
3/4 c. nuts

Cream butter and sugar. Add vanilla. Mix in flour and salt, stir in chopped nuts. Roll into small balls and bake in a moderate oven until light brown, about 10-12 minutes. You may wish to roll them in powdered sugar when they are cool.

Mrs. Peterson's Cookies

1 c. drippings OR lard
1 c. sugar
1/2 c. molasses
1 T. baking soda
1 t. ginger
1 egg, beaten
Pinch of salt
Flour

Cream drippings and sugar. Add molasses and egg and beat well. Add baking soda, ginger, salt and enough flour to make a soft dough. Drop by spoonfuls on greased cookie tin. Bake in a moderate oven for 15-20 minutes.

White Drop Cookies

1 c. sugar
1 c. shortening OR lard
2 eggs
1 t. vanilla
Pinch of salt
2 t. cream of tartar
1/2 t. baking soda
2 1/2 c. flour

Cream sugar and fat. Add eggs and beat well. Add vanilla, salt, cream of tartar, baking soda and flour. Drop and form with fork or by hand. Bake in moderate oven about 10 minutes.

Grandmother Gana's Cookies

1 c. butter
1 c. sugar
2 eggs
3 T. sweet milk
1 t. vanilla
1 t. baking soda
1 t. cream of tartar
2 1/2 c. flour

Beat together butter and sugar until creamy. Beat in eggs. Add milk and mix well. Add vanilla, baking soda, cream of tartar and flour. Roll out dough till it's quite thin. Cut into rounds and bake.

Plain Cookies

3/4 c. butter OR lard
1 1/2 c. sugar
3 eggs, beaten
1 T. milk
2 1/2 c. cake flour, sifted
2 T. baking powder

Cream butter and sugar; add beaten eggs. Add milk and beat well. Sift together flour and baking powder; stir into sugar/milk mixture. Roll out on a floured surface until thin. Cut into circles. Bake in a moderate oven till browned.

A Note About Molasses Cookies

Molasses cookies are very common, but they are not easy to make, the reason being that there is no rule you can work by which will answer in all cases. All molasses does not work alike. Some kinds will bear more water than others, and the weather has to be taken into consideration. You can use more water in cold weather that in warm, at times 1/2 water, 1/2 molasses. Be very careful and do not get dough too stiff and do not work more than necessary to mix.

Molasses Cookies

1 qt. molasses
1 gill water (1/2 c.)
2 oz. baking soda
1 c. lard
Flour

Put molasses, water, baking soda and lard in a large bowl; mix them together. Add flour enough to make a nice dough suitable to roll out and cut. Brush tops with milk or water. Bake in a moderate oven for about 10-15 minutes.

The Three Stooges performed an odd form of violent slapstick for movie-goers. The original Stooges were Larry Fine, Curly (Jerry) Howard and Moe Howard.

1935: O. D. McKee came up with the "Oatmeal Creme Pie." The two soft oatmeal cookies with a fluffy filling sold for 5 cents.

Molasses Cookies

1 c. sugar
1 c. shortening
1 c. molasses
2 eggs
1/2 c. sour milk
1 t. baking soda
1 t. salt
1 t. ginger

Beat sugar and shortening together till light and fluffy. Add remaining ingredients one at a time and beat after each addition. Roll out on a floured surface. Cut into any shape and bake in a moderate oven till done. From Mrs. Renolds.

Aunt Sally's Molasses Cookies

1 c. shortening OR lard
1 c. molasses
2 t. baking soda dissolved
   in 1/2 c. hot coffee
1 t. salt
1/2 t. nutmeg
1/4 t. ground cloves
3-4 c. flour

Cream shortening till fluffy. Add molasses; beat well. Add soda/ coffee, salt, nutmeg and cloves. Stir in enough flour to make a dough suitable for rolling out. Cut into any shape. Bake on greased cookie tins at 350 degrees for about 6 minutes. Watch them closely. Cool and frost with next recipe.

Cookie Frosting

1 envelope unflavored gelatin
3/4 c. water
3/4 c. sugar
3/4 c. powdered sugar
3/4 t. baking powder
1 t. vanilla

In a small saucepan soak gelatin in water until softened. Add sugar, bring to a boil and simmer 10 minutes. Take off fire, add powdered sugar. Beat hard until foamy. Add baking powder and vanilla and beat until very thick (this takes a long time.) Frost cookies; let dry.

Stone Jar Molasses Cookies

3/4 c. molasses
1/2 c. shortening OR lard
1 t. baking soda
2 1/4 c. flour
1 3/4 t. baking powder
1 t. salt
Dash of ginger
Dash of cinnamon

Heat molasses to boiling. Remove from fire and stir in shortening and baking soda. Mix together flour, baking powder, salt, ginger and cinnamon. Mix everything together. Chill 1 hour. Roll into balls and press with the bottom of a stoneware jar or drinking glass. Bake at 350 degrees for about 6 minutes.

Molasses-Ginger Snaps

1/2 c. butter
1/2 c. lard
1 c. sugar
1 c. molasses
1 lg T. ginger
1 t. cinnamon
1 t. ground cloves
1 t. allspice
1 t. baking soda in
  6 T. boiling water

Beat together butter, lard and sugar. Add molasses, spices, and soda/water. Stir in enough flour to make a stiff dough. Roll into pieces the size of hickory nuts in hand and flatten. Bake in a moderate oven for 10-15 minutes or until browned.

White Butter Cookies

1 c. butter
1 c. lard
3 c. sugar
2 eggs
1 c. sour cream
1/2 t. baking soda
2 t. vanilla
Flour

Cream butter, lard and sugar. Add eggs and sour cream, mix well. Sift together flour and baking soda; add to mixture. Mix well, roll out on floured board and cut into any shape. Bake in moderate oven for about 10-12 minutes or until lightly browned. Makes over 100 cookies, but is that enough?

Peanut Butter Cookies

1 c. sugar
1 c. brown sugar
1/2 c. butter
1/2 c. lard
2 eggs
2 T. baking soda
3/4 c. peanut butter
1 t. vanilla
2 c. flour

Cream sugars and fats until fluffy. Add eggs and beat well. Add baking soda, peanut butter and vanilla. Stir in flour. Roll with hands into balls. Place on greased cookie tin. Bake in a 375 degree oven for about 10-15 minutes. Flatten with fork before baking.

White Cookies

2 c. sugar
1 c. butter OR lard
1 c. sour cream
1 t. baking soda
  dissolved in water
2 eggs, beaten with
  nutmeg or lemon
About 3 1/2-4 c. flour

Cream together the sugar and lard or butter. Blend in well the sour cream and soda in water. Beat in eggs; add flour to make a soft dough. Roll out quite thin and bake at 350 degrees for about 8 minutes. This is one of Hana's favorite cookie recipes.

Date-Oatmeal Cookies

2 1/2 c. oatmeal
2 1/2 c. flour
1/4 c.+ butter
1 c. brown sugar
1 t. baking soda
Water

Filling
1 lb. dates
1 c. sugar
Chopped nuts
1 c. water

Beat together the butter and sugar. Add oatmeal, flour and baking soda and enough water so as to roll nicely. Mix with hands, divide dough in two. Roll out first the bottom crust. Add filling and cover with top crust. Bake in moderate oven. Cook dates, sugar, nuts and water in a saucepan. Cool before pouring onto dough. From Mollie.

Hana's Oatmeal Cookies

1/2 c. brn. sugar
1/2 c. sugar
1/2 c. lard
1 egg
1 t. vanilla
1 t. salt
3/4 c. flour
1 1/2 c. oatmeal
1/2 t. baking soda
1.2 c. nuts, chopped

Cream together the sugars and lard, till nice and fluffy. Add egg and beat well again. Add vanilla. Sift together salt, flour and baking soda. Add a little at a time to the sugar mixture. Stir in oatmeal and nuts. Drop by spoonfuls onto a baking sheet and bake in a 350 degree oven until light brown, about 10 minutes. Cool and store in cookie jar. Put the jar up out of the reach of the children!

White Sugar Cookies

1 c. butter
1/2 c. lard
1 1/2 c. sugar
1/2 c. sweet milk
2 eggs
1/2 t. baking soda
1 t. baking powder
4 c. flour

Cream together the butter, lard and sugar. Add the milk and eggs; beat well. Sift the flour with the baking soda and baking powder. Gradually add the flour mixture to the sugar mixture. Be sure to add just enough flour to make a soft dough. Roll out on a floured surface until thin. Cut with a cookie cutter or biscuit cutter. Bake at 375 degrees for about 8 minutes.

Many great film stars were entertaining Americans during the Depression Era. To name a few: W. C. Fields, the Marx Brothers, Laurel and Hardy, Mae West, Marlene Dietrich, Shirley Temple, Humphrey Bogart (Lauren Bacall didn't come on the scene until 1944), Bette Davis and Joan Crawford.

Rhubarb Sauce

2-3 c. rhubarb, chopped
1/2 c. water
1/2 c. sugar or more

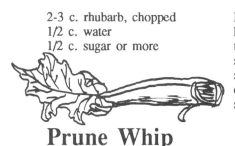

Put rhubarb and water into a kettle. (If the kettle is stained, it won't be when you're through.) Bring to a boil and cook a few seconds till tender. Stir in sugar. Chill and serve. It's good for breakfast too. This is even better if you put in about 1 c. of sliced strawberries.

Prune Whip

1 1/2 to 2 c. prunes
1/4 to 1/2 c. powdered sugar
1 t. lemon juice
2 egg whites,
    beaten stiff

Cook prunes until soft and run them through a fine sieve to get 1 c. pulp. Chill. Fold together pulp, sugar, lemon juice and egg whites. Pile lightly into serving bowls and chill. "If you can get prunes inside your kids this way, you're doing better than I am. Try some sweetened whip cream on top. It may help." -Grandma Signe

Apple Cottage Pudding

6 to 10 apples
1/2 c. milk
1 T. butter, melted
1 c. flour
1/2 c. sugar
1 t. Royal baking powder
1 t. vanilla

Peel, core and slice apples thin. Put apples in a buttered tin. Mix together milk, butter, flour, sugar, baking powder and vanilla. Pour batter over apples and bake in a moderate oven till done, about 45 minutes. Serve with cream or lemon sauce. This is good with other fruits, too.

1939: Movie-goers fell in love with Dorothy and her friends in "The Wizard of Oz," starring Judy Garland, Ray Bolger, Jack Haley, Bert Lahr, Margaret Hamilton and Frank Morgan as Oz. Two silent versions of the book by Frank Baum had been produced in 1910 and 1924, but the sound, music and the marvelous change from black-and-white to Technicolor delighted audiences then as it does now.

Marion Michael Morrison first appeared in the film "Salute" in 1929. He acted in 63 film movies from 1930-1939, an incredible statistic. Perhaps his most memorable film of the decade was "Stagecoach," 1939. Figure it out yet? You're right - he's John Wayne.

Egg Pudding

1/4 c. butter
1/2 c. flour
1/4 c. sugar
1 pt. milk
1 t. vanilla
5 eggs, separated

Melt butter, sift flour and sugar and add to butter; stir in milk. Cook for five minutes. Remove from fire and add beaten egg yolks. Add vanilla. Fold in carefully the beaten egg whites. Place pudding dish in a pan of water and bake for about forty minutes. Serve with any hard sauce.

Any Hard Sauce

1/3 c. butter
1 c. powdered sugar
   OR brown sugar
1/2 t. vanilla
Nutmeg

Cream butter until fluffy; add sugar gradually, beating well after each addition. Add vanilla. Serve over pudding or cake; sprinkle with a little nutmeg. You can add a little grated orange rind.

Fred Astaire and Ginger Rogers first danced their way into the hearts of Americans in "Flying Down to Rio," produced in 1933. Their grace and artistry is appreciated and as yet unequalled. Together they created dance that was delightfully magical, and audiences loved their performances.

Miscellaneous Recipes

The cook was a good cook,
as cooks go;
and as cooks go,
she went.

-Saki (H. H. Munroe)

141

Sachets

Mix all ingredients together in a covered jar. Let it set for a week or so before making into sachets.

2 c. juniper berries (cedar or balsam needles)
1 c. peppermint leaves
1 c. winterberry leaves
1/4 c. spearmint leaves
1 t. allspice
3/4 T. orrisroot
3 drops eucalyptus oil (optional)

1/2 c. geranium leaves (scented)
1/2 c. lemon verbena
1/2 c. dried lilacs
2 c. rose petals
1/2 t. orrisroot

2 c. rose petals
1 c. sweet lavender
1/4 c. basil
1 vanilla bean
1/4 t. cinnamon
1/8 t. ground cloves
1/8 t. nutmeg
1/2 t. orrisroot

Fragrant Rose Jar

1 pt. dried rose petals
1/4 oz. orris root
2 t. ginger
2 t. nutmeg
2 t. allspice
4 T. dried lemon verbena
4 T. dried lavender
Coarse salt
Grain alcohol

Pack thoroughly dried rose petals in a jar, sprinkling each layer with salt. Cover and let stand two weeks to a month. Then, blend spices and herbs in a large bowl. Add petals from the jar and mix well. Return mixture to jar, cover, and let rest for another month. When ready for use, shake jar well and add a few drops of alcohol.

1934: *During the drought, and consequent lack of pasture and/or hay, some farmers had to resort to feeding their cows thistles, which kept the herd alive, but caused a great number of arguments among family members as to who was to clean out the barn!*

Recipe for Chronic Cough

One pint each of lemon juice, olive oil, and extracted honey. One fresh egg. Put the lemon juice into a fruit jar or large-mouthed bottle. Wash egg and drop it <u>unbroken</u> into the lemon juice. In about 24 hours the shell of the egg will be dissolved. Then remove the tough inside skin being careful to leave every particle of the shell in the lemon juice. Beat all together. Warm it enough to mix well, and bottle. Keep in a cool place. Dose: a teaspoonful frequently.

A Cure for Pneumonia

Take 6-10 onions, according to size, and chop fine. Put in a skillet over a hot fire. Then add about the same quantity of rye meal and vinegar, enough to make a thick paste. In the meantime stir it thoroughly, letting it simmer 5-10 minutes. Then put it in a cotton bag large enough to cover the lungs, and apply to the chest as hot as the patient can bear. When this gets cool apply another and thus continue by reheating the poultices, and in a few hours the patient will be out of danger. This simple remedy has never failed in this too often fatal malady. Usually four applications will do, but continue always until perspiration starts freely from the chest.

Ant Poison

Dissolve one pound of sugar in one quart of water. Add 125 grains of arsenate of soda (10 cents worth.) Boil, strain, and cool. Add a few drops honey. Saturate small sponges in this syrup and place where the ants can have ready access to them.

Dyspeptic Bread

1 pt. flour (2 c.)
1 t. salt
4 t. baking powder
Milk & water

Sift dry ingredients. Mix to a soft dough with the milk and water. Knead 2 minutes, turn into a greased pan, let rise 10 minutes and bake slowly for 40 minutes. This bread can be eaten by those with weak digestion who can not assimilate bread prepared with yeast.

Wrinkle Cream

1 oz. white wax
2 oz. strained honey
2 oz. lily bulb juice

Melt ingredients together, cool. Apply to the face every night and it is said your wrinkles will disappear.

Mayonnaise Moisturizer

1 egg
1 c. salad oil
2 T. lemon juice

Blend egg and oil slowly; add vinegar. Apply to face and leave on for 1/2 hour. Remove with warm water.

Oatmeal Cleaner

2-3 T. oatmeal
Water

Grind oatmeal to a powder. Mix with water to make a paste. Gently rub onto face and neck. Rinse with warm, then cool water.

Milk Cleanser

1 T. milk
1/8 t. oil
1/8 t. honey

Mix ingredients well. Apply to face, blot off with damp cloth. Especially good for dry skin.

Hair Setting Lotion

1 c. flax seed
3 c. water

Simmer seeds and water together for a few minutes. Strain and thin to desired consistency.

Vinegar Hair Rinse

1 t. cider vinegar
1 qt. water

Mix together. After shampooing, use as a final rinse to make your hair shine.

Hair-Darkening Rinse

1 qt. water
1/3 c. sage leaves

Pour boiling water over sage and steep for 2 hours. Strain, pour over hair. After 1/2 hour, rinse.

Hard Soap

7 lbs. tallow
3 lbs. rosin
2 lbs. potash
6 gal. water

Mix ingredients; boil 3-5 hours. Pour into wash tub; let stand overnight. Cut into bars and lay in the sun 2-3 days to harden. This will last an ordinary family a year and save on money spent for soap.

> Red, White and Blue
> Girls must on their wedding day
> Have for luck, the old folks say,
> Something old and something new,
> Something borrowed and something blue.
> So when fair Marguerite was led
> Down the rose-strewn aisle to wed,
> She had followed to the end
> The rule that luck should her attend:
> Borrowed blushes on her face
> That the hue of love should grace;
> Bridal trousseau very new;
> The groom was old and she was blue.

Yesterday Belongs to the Past

Every joy which comes to you is a jewel which should be carefully placed in the jewel casket of the mind. But the thefts, the disappointments, the mistakes should be left with their own hour and day. Yesterday belongs distinctly to the past. The failures which belong to it are perished. It is wicked, inhuman to dig up the remnants of each and rehash it today. Half the failures made by both men and women are brought about by dwelling on other past failures. Half the miseries of both heart and mind are repeated because they are not left to the past. No man or woman can possibly live properly today if they spend time in living over the yesterday. Every well-balanced man and woman does each day that which he believes to be right. When tomorrow comes let today enjoy the peace of the past.

Recipe for Preserving Children

Take one grassy field, 1/2 dozen children, 3 small dogs, a pinch of a brook and some pebbles. Mix the children and dogs well together and put them in the field, stirring constantly. Pour the brook over the pebbles. Sprinkle the field with flowers, spread over all a deep blue sky, and bake in a hot sun. When brown, remove and set away to cool in a bath tub.

Odo-Ro-No promised their product would stop "Armhole Odor." The ad said you could send 8 cents for generous-sized bottles of both Instant Odorono and Regular Odorono, and a leaflet on complete underarm dryness.

146

Light After Darkness

Light after darkness, Gain after loss,
Strength after suffering, Crown after cross,
Sweet after bitter, Song after sigh,
Home after wandering, Praise after cry.
Sheaves after sowing, Sun after rain.
Sight after mystery, Peace after pain.
Joy after sorrow, Calm after blast,
Rest after weariness, Sweet rest at last.
Near after distant, Gleam after gloom,
Love after loneliness, Life after tomb.
After long agony, Rapture of bliss,
Right was the pathway leading to this.

Some Things to Remember about Milk

1. MILK is the chief food for lime which builds strong bones and teeth.
2. MILK contains the vitamins which make you grow.
3. MILK gives you energy and pep.
4. MILK builds your muscle.
5. MILK strengthens your nerves and is conducive to long life and happiness.

"THE MILK WAY IS THE HEALTH WAY"

--FOLLOW IT--

The general drought and the Dust Bowl in Oklahoma, Texas and Kansas reminded people of the old southern melody, "It Ain't Gonna Rain No Mo'," and they sang it constantly. Although the original song dates back at least to the 1870's, the sheet music was published in 1927. "How in the heck can I wash my neck?...How in the dickens can I wash my chickens if it ain't gonna rain no mo'?" were certainly appropriate questions for those extremely dry times. And it was one of those songs that people could expand on and make up lyrics to, which they did: "How in the helly can I wash my belly?"..."How in the tub can I rub-a-dub-dub?"..."How on earth can I wash my girth?"..."How in the hell can the old folks tell?"...Hey, make up your own, it's fun!

Before electricity came to rural America, and when folks couldn't afford to have "the ice man cometh," they would put milk and cream into buckets and lower them deep into the well. It was cool down there, even on hot days, and this provided them with at least some refrigeration.

Some Good Tips for the Newlyweds

Spend less than you earn.

Make a budget.

Keep a record of expenditures.

Have a bank account.

Carry LIFE insurance.

Insure your house and contents.

Own your own home.

Pay your bills promptly.

Share with others.

Avoid waste in every form.

Realize the responsibility of the marriage
relationship - bear and forebear.

Wives must cook well if they would keep
their husbands.

Husbands should confide in their wives,
and the wives should take an interest
in their husbands problems.

Wives must be neat. If their husbands like
the latest styles, the wives should govern
themselves accordingly.

Husbands should see that their wives get
plenty of entertainment. They should take
them to movies, for auto rides, walks and
swims, or whatever the wife likes.

If there has been a quarrel, kiss and make up
before going to sleep. Never let such
feelings last overnight.

Don't try to keep up with the Joneses.

Household Hints & Measures

"In baiting a mouse trap with cheese,
Always leave room for the mouse."

-Saki (H. H. Munroe)

"Handiest thing in the house"

*Every day
we find
some new need
for*
Vaseline
REG. U. S. PAT. OFF.
PETROLEUM JELLY

THOUSANDS of housewives — when asked how they use "Vaseline" Petroleum Jelly — answered with enthusiasm:

"There are dozens of ways in which it helps us."

"It's the handiest thing in the house."

"Every day we find some new need for it — for first-aid uses, for certain beauty purposes many women overlook, for household lubricating, cleaning, polishing."

How true this last statement, particularly, is. For "Vaseline" Jelly is a unique product unlike anything else you can buy, more useful for so many purposes than any similar product, and familiar to the whole world because of its many, many years of usefulness.

Each family ought to have several jars or tubes on hand. Keep a special tube for the baby; a jar for your own toilet use; a jar in the kitchen ready for emergencies; a tube in garage or workshop or barn or club locker for the men of the family.

Here are some of the ways in which "Vaseline" Jelly helps other women:

First Aid Uses

Minor Cuts — wash under running water and apply "Vaseline" Jelly.

More serious wounds — sterilize with an approved antiseptic, dress with "Vaseline" Jelly and bandage lightly.

Burns — Cover the burned area with "Vaseline" Jelly, spread on clean linen or gauze. Change dressing daily.

Scalds — Cover the scalded area with "Vaseline" Jelly, spread on clean linen or gauze. Change dressing daily.

Blisters — Prick the edge of the blister with a sterilized needle, press out the water, and dress with "Vaseline" Jelly.

Sores — Apply "Vaseline" Jelly at frequent intervals.

Bumps and Bruises — Apply cold compresses, immediately, then dress with "Vaseline" Jelly.

Head Colds — Place a little "Vaseline" Jelly in each nostril when retiring. For tickling coughs take a teaspoonful internally as required.

Toilette Uses

For scalp and hair — To dress hair, make it shiny, help hold the wave, spread a tiny bit of "Vaseline" Jelly over the palms of the hands, and apply to the hair. Then brush briskly. To treat the scalp, part the hair, lock by lock, massage the scalp at the part with "Vaseline" Jelly on the finger tips. Leave on over night, then shampoo.

To shape the eyebrows — Apply a bit of "Vaseline" Jelly with the finger tip and shape with an eyebrow brush.

To encourage the eyelashes — Apply "Vaseline" Jelly with a tiny brush and leave on over night.

For chapped lips and skin — Apply to the lips several times a day. Spread a thin layer over chapped skin and leave on all night.

To beautify hands — If the hands are rough and cracked, massage with "Vaseline" Jelly, and wear soft silk or cotton gloves over night. If the hands are grimy from manual work,

massage with "Vaseline" Jelly and wash with a non-irritating soap. If the grime has got into the cracks of the hands, leave the "Vaseline" Jelly on over night and wear gloves. This treatment makes the hands soft, and keeps the cuticle of the nails firm.

Household Uses

To prevent rust — Pots, waffle irons, the iron parts of the kitchen stove etc., can be kept free from rust by coating with "Vaseline" Jelly when not in use.

Nickel and aluminum polish — With "Vaseline" Jelly you can restore the bright finish.

Squeaky hinges — "Vaseline" Jelly relieves the squeak in a jiffy.

Screens — Prevent screens from getting rusty by rubbing with a cloth in which a bit of "Vaseline" Jelly has been rubbed.

Washing machines — Use "Vaseline" Jelly in the grease cup. It won't drip.

Electric fans — Use "Vaseline" Jelly in the grease cup.

Victrola — Lubricate with "Vaseline" Jelly. So easy to use.

For fine furniture — Rub "Vaseline" Jelly in thoroughly with a soft cloth. Imparts a fine finish and preserves the wood. Old furni-

ture needs this constant oiling.

To dress leather — Rub well with a soft cloth and "Vaseline" Jelly.

Shoe cleaning — "Vaseline" Jelly is the best dressing for patent leather shoes. For scuffed black satin shoes, slick down with a tiny bit of "Vaseline" Jelly. Takes off that scuffed look all children's shoes get so easily. Also restores the softness of leather when shoes have been soaked.

If you are interested in keeping these and other uses for handy reference, write Dept. W 5-27, Chesebrough Manufacturing Company, 17 State St., New York, for new booklet of uses.

"Vaseline" Petroleum Jelly is on sale everywhere in bottles, tubes and tins.

And remember when you buy that the trademark "Vaseline" on the package gives you the assurance that you are getting the genuine product of the Chesebrough Manufacturing Company, Cons'd.

Mildew in white clothes may be removed by soaking for a short time in a pail of water to which has been added a heaping teaspoon of chloride of lime. Then hang in the sun. Repeat if necessary.

When frying potatoes, etc., try chopping with an empty baking powder can instead of a knife. You will find it much more handy and quicker.

Try greasing cake and bread pans with a small, five-cent paint brush. Keep grease in round tin can; cut hole in cover and insert handle of brush when not in use. It is then always ready for use and does not soil the handle.

To prevent cake from burning when using new tins, butter the new tins well and place them in a moderate oven for fifteen minutes. After this, the cake may be cooked in them without danger of burning.

When heating iron with gas stove, place a lid from the coal stove over the gas burners and place the irons over this. The irons will always be clean and heat much better than if they are put directly over the gas flame.

To clean plaster of paris figurines, use toilet soap suds and a shaving brush. Rinse well. Dipping them in a strong solution of alum water will give them the appearance of alabaster.

To preserve gilt frames, cover them when new with a coat of white varnish. All specks can then be washed off with water without injury.

To keep lemons, put them in water. Change once a week. Will keep a long time this way.

Do not use towels in wiping razor blades, have a cloth for that purpose.

Perspiration causes silk stockings to rot, so do not allow them to dry before rinsing them.

The backyard should be as clean as the front garden.

Buy canned goods by the dozen; soap by the box.

Keep a plant and flowers in your kitchen.

Keep your basement dry; large windows are desireable.

Map our your next day's work.

Never dry woodenware near the stove.

Place your broom in a tub of water, occasionally.

Graniteware is easiest to keep clean.

Care of the Kitchen Floor

A linoleum covered floor is the most easily kept clean. The hardwood floor is the next best. Anything spilled should be wiped up at once. Grease spots on wood or stone should be covered with flour, starch or powdered chalk, to absorb the grease. Or if you pour cold water on the grease, as soon as it is spilled, to harden it, the greater part may then be scraped off. Sweep the floor thoroughly once a day. With care it will not need washing or scrubbing oftener than once a week.

Care of the Hardwood Floor

Never use water on a hardwood floor. Wipe it with a cloth moistened with very little kerosene - a teaspoon or two to begin with, and as much more when that has evaporated. Rub hard with another cloth until the wood is perfectly dry. Window sills and all hardwood finish should be cleaned in the same way.

Cleaning Paint

Take a little whiting on a clean, damp cloth and rub it on the surface to be cleaned. Take care not to let drops of water trickle down the paint. Wash off with a second cloth and clean water. Wipe dry with a third cloth. Clean a little at a time, leaving the cleaned part dry before going on.

Care of Sink

Neglect of the sink causes bad odors and attracts water-bugs and roaches. Keep it at all times free from scraps. When the dishes have been washed, scour it with a good scouring soap. Wipe the woodwork and tiling. Wash strainer, soap dish and other sink utensils. Wash the cloth. Scrub the draining board and rinse the sink.

Special Instructions

Do not put knife handles in water. Water discolors and cracks ivory and bone handles, and may loosen wooden ones. After washing knives, scour them with bath brick.

Be careful not to wet the cogs of a Dover egg-beater. Wash the lower part, and wipe off the handles with a damp cloth. Water washes the oil from the cogs, making the beater hard to turn.

Dip glasses into hot water, so that they will be wet inside and outside at the same time.

Silver and glass are brightest if wiped directly from clean, hot suds, without being rinsed.

Cooking Hints and Notes

Before grinding dates, figs, prunes or raisins, squeeze some lemon juice through the grinder. The fruits won't stick, and the grinder will be easier to clean.

Adding water to eggs instead of milk will make scrambled eggs fluffier. Add about 1 tablespoon of water per egg.

A few drops of water added to eggs will also make them easier to beat.

Pour orange juice over raisins, store covered in a cool place for several hours. The raisins will absorb the juice and you'll have a new flavor treat for your salads, cereals, cookies or snacks.

Keep bugs out of your cupboards and canisters this way: put a bay leaf in your flour, pasta or other grain container. Sprinkle some pieces of bay leaf in your cupboard drawers and on the shelves where baking and cooking ingredients are stored.

To keep milk from sticking to the pan when you heat it, rinse the pan with cold water first.

Five parts flour and one part cornstarch makes a good pastry flour for pies.

Bits of butter or lard dotted near the edge of apple or fruit pies prevents the juice from running our while baking.

More juice can be squeezed from a lemon if it has been heated a little in the oven first. If the rind is to be used, grate it before heating.

To beat the whites of storage eggs, add a few grains of salt.

When baking cakes, cookies or doughnuts, if sour milk is called for and is not on hand, add about one T. of vinegar to one cup of sweet milk and let stand two minutes.

Substitutions

1 lb. cheese = 5 cups grated

1 c. chopped nutmeats = 1/4 pound

11 finely crumbled graham crackers = 1 cup

1 lb. seedless raisins = 2 3/4 cups

1 lb. pitted dates = 2 1/2 cups

3 1/2 lbs. dressed chicken = 2 c. cooked & diced

A "dash" = less than 1/8 t.

1 gill = 1/2 cup

2 T. fat = 1 ounce

1 c. fat = 1/2 pound

2 c. butter = 1 pound

1 c. fat + 1/2 t. salt = 1 c. butter

2 c sugar = 1 pound

2 1/4 c. packed brown sugar = 1 pound

1 c. packed brown sugar = 1 c. granulated sugar

3 1/2 c. powdered sugar = 1 pound

4 c. sifted all purpose flour = 1 pound

1 oz. bitter chocolate = 1 square

3 T. cocoa + 1 T. butter = 1 oz. bitter chocolate

1 c. egg whites = 8-10 whites

1 c. egg yolks = 12-14 yolks

1 T. cornstarch = 2 T. flour for thickening

1 c. whipping cream = 2-2 1/2 c. whipped cream

1 c. evaporated milk = 1/2 c. evaporated + 1/2 c. water

1 lemon = 2-3 T. juice + 2 t. rind

1 orange = 6-8 T. juice

1 c. uncooked rice = 3-4 c. cooked rice

1 c. uncooked macaroni = 2-2 1/4 c. cooked macaroni

Oven Chart

Very Slow Oven = 250 to 300 degrees

Slow Oven = 300 to 325 degrees

Moderate Oven = 325 to 375 degrees

Medium Hot Oven = 375 to 400 degrees

Hot Oven = 400 to 450 degrees

Very Hot Oven = 450 to 500 degrees

A Guide to Herbs and Spices

ALLSPICE: Allspice is native to the West Indies and Central America. It resembles a mixture of cloves, cinnamon and nutmeg. Allspice is used in marinades, (particularly for game,) in curries, spice cakes, sweet vegetable dishes, for pickling fruits and vegetables and, of course, for lutefisk.

ANISE: One of the sweetest-smelling herbs, anise is also a member of the carrot family. It is found primarily in Egypt, Greece and Turkey. The seeds and leaves both have a sweet, licorice-like flavor. Its principal use is in making liqueurs, but anise seed is also used in cookies, cakes and breads as well as in certain sauces, sausages and cabbage slaws.

BASIL: A powerful herb with a heady aroma that is native to the Near East. Basil can be used with most vegetables, especially tomatoes, green beans, broccoli, eggplant, artichokes, peas, zucchini and spinach. It's also good in green salads, vegetable soups, egg dishes and pastas, meat, fish and poultry dishes.

BAY LEAF: Also called "laurel," it comes from an evergreen shrub-tree native to the Mediterranean region. Its heavy flavor may overpower foods. It is used most often in cooking hearty meat and fish dishes and is essential for a bouquet garni.

CARAWAY SEEDS: They come from a biennial herb with lacy foliage grown primarily in the Netherlands. The brown, crescent-shaped seeds ripen after the plant dies. According to myth, caraway vents theft or infidelity and cures hysteria. Caraway seeds lighten the flavor of heavy foods such as pork and sauerkraut. Use them in breads or with vegetables such as carrots, green beans and potatoes.

CARDAMON: Cardamon is native to India. Only the dried ripe seeds of the cardamon plant are used. Pungent and aromatic, cardamon is similar to ginger but more subtle. It is used in Indian curry dishes and in Scandinavian pastries.

CHERVIL: Chervil leaves resemble those of parsley. It is easy to grow in an herb garden. A member of the carrot family, it has spicy overtones and a slight flavor of licorice. In France it is considered a blending herb. Because of its delicate nature, it can be used generously. Use it with cream cheese or cottage cheese and in omelets, soups or fish dishes.

CINNAMON: One of the oldest spices known. Most cinnamon comes from a cassia tree. Use this sweet spicy flavoring in seasoning meats or meat cooked with fruit. It also enhances carrots, squash, eggplant, tomatoes and baked goods.

CLOVES: Unopened flower buds of an evergreen tree, cloves are cultivated in Indonesia and Madagascar. They are potent, so use cloves sparingly in combination with bay, cinnamon, ginger or curry. Use in spicy meat, fish or poultry dishes and in baked goods.

CUMIN: Cumin seeds come from a low-growing annual herb, of the carrot family, native to the Mediterranean area. Cumin, a symbol of greed to the ancient Greeks, has a taste similar to that of caraway seed. Use it in Mexican or Indian dishes or to season robust meat and vegetable dishes. The Dutch and Swiss use it to flavor cheese.

DILL: A relative of the carrot family, the leaf and the seed of dill are used in salads and with most vegetables, fish and shellfish. It also complements eggs and light cream cheeses.

FENNEL: Almost all of the plant is edible. The seed has a sweet taste with a slight hint of licorice. Use it in breads, sausages, spicy meat mixtures, salads and soups.

GINGER: One of the first Oriental spices known in Europe. The fresh root is used in cookies, breads or spice cakes, curried dishes or pot roasts.

MARJORAM: An aromatic herb of the mint family, marjoram is native to the Mediterranean but is now widely cultivated around the world. It's closely related to oregano but is sweeter and milder. Use it sparingly in soups, sauces, stuffings and stews; it also goes well with eggplant, summer squash, tomatoes and mushrooms.

MINT: Spearmint is the most common garden mint. It may be used with beef, veal, fish and lamb, or with beans, carrots, eggplant, peas, potatoes, spinach, and green salads. Crush dried or fresh leaves just before adding them to a dish.

NUTMEG: Nutmeg is the seed from the tropical nutmeg tree. The outer skin-covering of the seed is used for mace. Nutmeg and mace have similar flavors, but mace is more intense and pungent. Use it in custards, pies and cheese dishes or sparingly in cream sauces and meat dishes.

OREGANO: Also known as wild marjoram. Because of its potent flavor, use it sparingly. It compliments almost all tomato dishes and goes well with most vegetables and with meats or stews.

PAPRIKA: The dried, finely ground pods of a sweet pepper plant. It can be decidedly hot to pleasantly mild. It can be used for adding color, or for flavoring meat dishes such as stews and goulash.

PARSLEY: Most often thought of as a garnish, parsley is delicious when used in large quantities as a separate seasoning. It is used in most herb blends and can add a fresh taste to meats, soups, stews and vegetable dishes.

PEPPER: Both black and white pepper come from the tiny berries of a vine native to the East Indies. White pepper is made by soaking black peppercorns and removing the dark outer coating; it is sometimes preferred for use in white sauces.

POPPY SEEDS: They have a mild flavor vaguely similar to that of walnuts, but poppy seeds are most often used for their texture. The slate-blue seeds of the poppy plant are from another variety than that which yields opium. It is estimated that there are 900,000 poppy seeds to the pound. They are used in breads, rolls, cookies, pie crusts, and cake or to season noodles or vegetables.

ROSEMARY: Native to the Mediterranean, rosemary is sometimes used there is garden landscaping. The mint-family herb grows 2-6 feet high with narrow leaves that look like pine needles. Use a little rosemary with orange sections, in dumplings and biscuits or in poultry stuffings. It's also good in pea soup and in stews, with beans, peas, spinach and zucchini, lamb and pork.

SAGE: Sage is now widely cultivated in California and other western states. This fragrant herb has a slightly bitter taste and is a versatile seasoning used in stuffings, sausage and with poultry, pork and veal. Use it with cheese dishes or with lima beans, onions, tomatoes and eggplant.

TARRAGON: A classic herb used in French cooking. The flavor is spicy, sharp and aromatic with overtones of licorice and mint. It is essential to bernaise sauce and adds a nice touch to tartar sauce. It also is used with poultry, fish and eggs.

THYME: Thyme is a strong-flavored herb with a clove-like taste. Use it sparingly in herb blends, creamy soups and fish chowders, and in all kinds of meat, fish, game and poultry dishes. Onions, carrots, beets, mushrooms, beans, potatoes and tomatoes also go well with thyme.

INDEX

Salmon, con't -
  Mrs. Gilbert's Salmon Mold, 68
Sauce -
  Any Hard, 139
  Rhubarb, 138
Sausage -
  Country Pork, 40
  Venison, 54
Saw Mill Beef, 47
Scalloped Rhubarb, 131
Scrambled Eggs, 6
Scrapple, 47
Seven Min. Frosting, 123
Shirred Eggs, 4
Shrub -
  Cherry, 22
  Raspberry, 22
Simple Dressing, 91
Slumgullion, 48
Soap, Hard, 146
Soft Ginger Bread, 102
Soup -
  Amber, 34
  Bean, 36
  Beef Broth, 35
  Bouillon, 35
  Caramel for, 34
  Chicken, 29
  Chicken Stock, 29
  Clam Broth, 32
  Clam Chowder, 31
  Cream of Celery, 33
  Cream of Oyster, 31
  Cream of Tomato, 32, 35
  Fish Chowder, 65
  Garden, 36
  Ma's Pea, 31
  Ma's Turkey, 32
  Mutton Broth, 32
  Oxtail, 34
  Peanut, 34
  Poor Man's, 30
  Turkey, 29
  Vegetable, 30, 33
Southern -
  Baked Ham, 43
  Egg Bread, 104
  Fried Chicken, 59

Spanish -
  Omelet, 3
  Rice, 77
Spicy Sweet Potatoes, 80
Sponge Cake, 121
Spoon Bread, 96
Spruce Beer, 25
Squash -
  Baked, 77
  Baked Winter, 79
  Zucchini Summer, 79
Steamed -
  Brown Bread, 106
  Graham Pudding, 129
Steeped Coffee, 17
Stew -
  Beef, 36
  Hunter's, 49
  Irish, 52
  Italian, 46
  Rabbit, 53
Stewed -
  Corn, 77
  Squirrels, 53
Stock, Beef, 29
Stock, Chicken, 29
Stone Jar Molasses Cookies, 135
Streusel Crumbs, 103
Stuffed -
  Calf's Heart, 45
  Peppers, 48
  Mushrooms, 80
  Roast Raccoon, 50
  Shoulder of Mutton, 43
  Tomato Salad, 87
Stuffing -
  Turkey, 60
  Wild Rice, 61
Sunflower Salad, 87
Swedish -
  Kaldomar, 40
  Rull Sylta, 44
  Sausage, 39
Sweet Breads, Fried, 45
Sweet Rolls, 98
Swiss Eggs, 7
Swiss Steak, 46, 50

T

Tea, Making, 22
Tomato (es) -
  And Lima Beans, 83
  Baked, 79
  Bisque, 30
  Cream of, Soup, 32, 35
  Creole, 77
  Fresh Tomato Fry, 74
  Jellied, 85
  Soup, 32
  Stuffed Salad, 87
  With Mayonnaise, 79
Turbot, 67
Turkey -
  Roast & Dressing, 60
  Soup, 29
  Stuffing, 60
Turnips, Hashed, 78

U

Uncle John's Navy Hash, 40

V

Veal -
  Collops, 42
  Croquettes, 42
  Cutlets, 42
  Ham Pot Pie, 39
  Loaf, 41, 49
Vegetable Soup, 30, 33, 35
Venison Roast, 51
Venison Sausage, 54
Vinegar Hair Rinse, 145
Vinegar, Raspberry, 21

W

Waffles, 9, 10
  Cereal, 11
  Cornmeal, 11
Whipped Cream Dessert, 127
White -
  Butter Cookies, 136
  Cookies, 136
  Drop Cookies, 133
  Soup, 35

White, con't
  Sugar Cookies, 137
Whole Wheat Biscuits, 105
Wild Rice Stuffing, 61

Wine -
  Blackberry, 24
  Communion, 24
  Dandelion, 23
  Elderberry Blossom, 24
  Raisin, 23
Wrinkle Cream, 145

Z

Zucchini Summer Squash, 79

NOTES

NOTES

NOTES

NOTES